Rights of Women
A Guide to the Most Important United Nations Treaties on Women's Human Rights

Published by the International Women's Tribune Centre
New York, 1998. 148 pages

RIGHTS OF WOMEN

Editors:	Vicki J. Semler, Anne S. Walker, Leonora Wiener, Tina Johnson, Jane Garland Katz
Writers:	Dianne Otto, Leonora Wiener, Joan Ross Frankson, Stephanie Banuelos, Alice Mastrangelo-Gittler, Maggie Range, Vicki J. Semler, Anne S. Walker, Jane Garland Katz, Tina Johnson, Susan Davis
Legal Consulting Team:	Dianne Otto, Valerie Oosterveld, Clarence Dias, Jane Connors (UN/DAW), Office of the UN High Commissioner for Human Rights (NY)
Readers:	Rosalind Harris, Alice Quinn, Shulamith Koenig, Ilana Landsberg-Lewis (UNIFEM)
Researchers:	Sharon Taylor, Claire Hochachka, Leyla Gülçür, Meera Singh, Mischa Mills
Production Team:	Anne S. Walker, Tina Johnson, Sarah Sills
Line Illustrations by:	Anne S. Walker, Sarah Sills, Grace Jung, Laurel Douglas
Book Design and Cover by:	Sarah Sills

Copyright © 1998 by the International Women's Tribune Centre
All rights reserved

Printed in the United States of America
Price: $15.95

Library of Congress Cataloging-in-Publication Data
Rights of women: a guide to the important United Nations treaties for women's human rights
    p.   cm.
Includes bibliographical references.
ISBN 0-945006-00-4
1. International Women's Tribune Centre.
  K.644.R54 1998
  341.4'81--dc21

                                              98-12639
                                                  CIP

This is the 2nd Edition of Rights of Women in English.
1st edition (English) -------------1982   Derechos de la Mujer (Spanish) ---------1987
2nd edition (English) -----------1998   Droits de la Femme (French)------------1989

Rights of Women is available from:
Women, Ink.
777 United Nations Plaza
New York, NY 10017, USA
Tel: (1-212) 687-8633
Fax: (1-212) 661-2704
E-mail: ‹wink@womenink.org›
Web Site: ‹http://www.womenink.org›
  –Credit cards accepted–

TABLE OF CONTENTS

INTRODUCTION 1
   Women and Human Rights: Why do we Need this Book? 1
   Who the Book is For and How it Might be Used 3

SECTION 1 • UNDERSTANDING CONVENTIONS 5
   Human Rights Conventions.....Why Are They Important to Women? 6
   What is a Human Rights Convention? 7
   How Does a Convention Become Law? 8
   How Are Conventions Enforced? 9
   Other Enforcement Procedures 13
   UN Institutions that Protect Human Rights 14
   Where to Find UN Human Rights Conventions 15
   Form for Documenting Violations of Women's Human Rights 17

SECTION 2 • KNOW YOUR RIGHTS 19
   Women and Human Rights 20
   Your Human Rights and the Laws that Protect Them 24
      •Women and Education 30
      •Women and Employment 33
      •Women and Marriage 38
      •Women Refugees 42
      •Sexual Exploitation and Trafficking 46
      •Women and Torture 52

SECTION 3 • DEVELOPING RIGHTS 55
   Redefining Women's Human Rights 56
      •Housing, Land and Property 60
      •Violence Against Women 62
      •Reproductive Rights 67
      •Environmental Rights 70
      •Women with Disabilities 73
      •Sexual Orientation Rights 76

SECTION 4 • TAKING ACTION 77
   Converting Words into Action 78
      •A Country Manual 79
      •A Tribunal: Making Women's Voices Heard 90
      •Information Tools: Building Human Rights Communities 103

SECTION 5 • RESOURCE KIT 125
   Ratification Charts/Convention Abbreviations 126
   United Nations Human Rights Conventions Chart 136
   Convention on the Elimination of All Forms of Discrimination Against Women (CEDAW) 137
   Anatomy of the Beijing Platform for Action 144
   IWTC and Women Ink. 146
   Women, Ink. Resources/Titles Mentioned in Rights of Women 147
   Women, Ink. Order Form 148

Produced by the International Women's Tribune Centre

Acknowledgements

To adequately acknowledge all the people who have played a role in the development of this edition of *Rights of Women* would be impossible. It builds on the experience, patience and perseverance of numerous individuals from a wide variety of countries with an equally wide and varied expertise—lawyers, journalists, professors and students, popular educators and community development workers. It has involved innumerable hours of discussion and debate, writing, field-testing and rewriting in a seemingly endless cycle, and we deeply appreciate all who have contributed their time, their vision and their skill. This also includes those involved in the field-testing of women's human rights training activities by women's groups and legal advisers both at IWTC and in Nepal and Uganda, even though training activities have not been included in this manual. These activities will form the core of a companion publication to *Rights of Women* due for completion in the coming year.

This manual builds on the work of three earlier editions. The first edition of *Rights of Women*, produced in 1982, was edited by Rosalind Harris. It profiled 44 international conventions, and included a worksheet for each one. In 1987, a substantially revised Spanish version entitled *Derechos de la Mujer* was produced by IWTC staff members Vicky Mejia Marulanda and Joanne Sandler, in collaboration with the Venezuelan Federation of Women Lawyers. This edition added a programme activity section that set the conventions within a larger context. IWTC's French edition, *Droits de la Femme*, followed in 1989, essentially as a translation and adaptation of the Spanish edition, with final editing by Vicky Mejia Marulanda, Maria Negroni and Sherazade Boualia. The feedback and evaluation of these materials was vital to the development of this current edition.

Resources are not developed in a vacuum and much of the work on *Rights of Women* has been influenced by the environment in which and the groups with whom IWTC has been privileged to work. In particular, mention should be made of IWTC's involvement in the preparatory process to the UN World Conference on Human Rights, Vienna 1993, and the global petition campaign against violations of women's human rights that, with the activities of women in every world region, culminated in a Global Tribunal on Women's Human Rights in Vienna. The planning and preliminary process for all these activities was undertaken in collaboration with the Center for Women's Global Leadership and a group of international NGOs all actively involved in the issue of women's human rights.

IWTC's work in the field of women's human rights has also been enriched by contact with women from every world region, and by participation in the meetings of the UN Commission on the Status of Women (CSW), the Committee on the Elimination of All Forms of Discrimination Against Women (CEDAW), and in the Beijing process. This includes the preparatory activities leading up to, as well as events and workshops that took place during the Fourth World Conference on Women and NGO Forum in Beijing, 1995.

We would also like to express our appreciation for the financial support for this project received from the following agencies and foundations:

- UN Fund for Population Activities;
- Swedish International Development Authority Division for Democratic Governance/Dept. for Democracy and Social Development;
- Department for International Development, United Kingdom;
- Ministry for Foreign Affairs, Finland;
- The Shaler Adams Foundation, USA.

The assistance of these agencies has made both the production of this manual and its free dissemination to individuals and groups in the Global South possible.

We also would like to take this opportunity to thank those agencies who give general support to IWTC but who are often not mentioned in the crediting of some projects. Without them, no projects would be possible. Support for the activities of IWTC during 1996-1998 has come from: The Netherlands Ministry for Foreign Affairs; Swedish International Development Authority, Gender Unit/Department for Policy and Legal Issues; Canadian International Development Agency; Ministry for Foreign Affairs, Denmark; Swiss Agency for Development and Cooperation; Australian Agency for International Development; United Methodist Church of the USA, Board of Global Ministries/Ministry of Women and Children; The Shaler Adams Foundation, USA; The Samuel Rubin Foundation, USA; and The Joselow Foundation, USA.

Anne S. Walker, Executive Director
Vicki J. Semler, Associate Director
International Women's Tribune Centre

Introduction

WOMEN AND HUMAN RIGHTS: WHY DO WE NEED THIS BOOK?

The struggle for women's human rights has gained enormous momentum during the past two decades, combining analysis and activism and giving birth to new organizations and coalitions, new laws, new learnings, and new levels of political activism, particularly in the legal arena. Beginning with the 1975 International Women's Year (IWY) World Conference and IWY Tribune in Mexico City, continuing through the women's world conferences and NGO Forums of 1980 (Copenhagen), 1985 (Nairobi), and the series of agenda-setting UN world conferences and NGO Forums of the 1990s that culminated in the 1995 Fourth World Conference on Women in Beijing, women have developed and discovered new skills and tools that they are now using to leverage for change on behalf of women's rights at global, country and community levels.

One tool that women are increasingly turning to in order to press forward their claims for justice are UN international conventions. These are the most powerful tools the UN has to offer civil society, yet they are much less well-known than the policy documents that emerge from world conferences, such as the Beijing Platform for Action. This *Rights of Women* manual seeks to address this issue by making conventions that are relevant to women more accessible. It is designed to assist its readers, particularly those working at grassroots or community level, to develop their own materials and undertake their own campaigns. People cannot participate in things they do not know about, and women cannot use international conventions unless they learn about them. Working effectively with international conventions is a process that requires an understanding of:

- what conventions exist
- how they can be used
- what national laws they relate to
- what the country's position is concerning the convention
- what is being done at national level (and who is doing it) to ensure compliance.

Human rights conventions relevant to the needs and concerns of women have been fought for and won, yet the major problem remains that many of them have still not been implemented. Given that the experience of women varies greatly from country to country and from region to region, it is still a fact that for the vast majority of women

> **As women lead they are changing leadership; as women organize, they are changing organizations.**
>
> —Mary Robinson, UN High Commissioner for Human Rights.

INTRODUCTION

both in the Global North and the Global South, there is a huge gap between women's human rights entitlements and the human rights that women and girls actually enjoy in their everyday lives.

This book therefore aims to encourage and inform the continuing struggle for women's human rights around the world. It focuses on those human rights that are guaranteed by human rights conventions, and how these conventions might be better realized. There are five sections, beginning with a general section on conventions, then moving to more focused sections on specific rights, ways of taking action, and availability of resources.

Section 1: "Understanding Conventions" provides an explanation of human rights conventions, how they work and why they are important to women. Also included is an explanation of the procedures for the enforcement of conventions, a description of the major United Nations institutions that protect human rights, where to find UN human rights conventions, and a form for documenting violations of women's human rights.

Section 2: "Know Your Rights" outlines the many human rights to which women are entitled. It also draws particular attention to some specific human rights that are of special importance to

CONVENTIONS CAN BE USED TO:

1. Pressure governments for more gender sensitive policies and legislation.

2. Hold governments accountable for commitments made.

3. Provide a legal basis for new interpretations or changes in existing national laws and/or the passage of new legislation.

4. Create an expanded human rights framework (and ultimately greater freedom) for women than that allowed within their own culture or under their own legal system.

5. Give legitimacy and visibility to campaigns that protest religious and/or culturally-based customs.

6. Provide access to a larger human rights community including legal recourse and advocacy groups.

7. Provide a common basis across national borders for the development of strategies and the exchange of experience using the common language and understandings of the international conventions. This is particularly useful with regards to the establishment of legal precedent.

8. Offer access to international legal bodies and related review and complaint procedures.

9. Provide a measuring stick to gauge the ability of governments to govern with justice.

INTRODUCTION

women, including: education, employment, equality in marriage, refugee rights, and protections from sexual exploitation, trafficking and torture.

Section 3: "Developing Rights" highlights some areas that women's human rights groups are fighting to have recognized as women's human rights. Included amongst these are: housing, land and property rights; the right to be protected against violence; reproductive rights; environmental rights; the rights of women with disabilities; and sexual orientation rights.

Section 4: Taking Action" focuses on action around women's human rights issues. Included are suggestions of ways to create a rights manual for your own country, to hold a women's human rights tribunal, and to use information tools for building human rights communities.

Section 5: "Resources Kit" includes: convention ratification charts; lists of United Nations human rights conventions; the Convention on the Elimination of All Forms of Discrimination Against Women (CEDAW); an illustrated outline and summary of the Beijing Platform for Action; and information on IWTC and Women, Ink. with a list and order form for Women, Ink. books.

WHO THE BOOK IS FOR AND HOW IT MIGHT BE USED

This book is for all women who want to participate in the struggle for women's human rights. It may be that you want to take action with respect to a particular human rights violation that you—or a friend—have experienced, or that you want to support other women in fighting for more general human rights protections. Whatever the reason, this book is for you in your work around women's human rights.

We have organized the book by specific human rights so that you will be able to find information about them more easily. For instance, you may want to know about your rights as a married woman. You would first turn to Section 2: "Know Your Rights" to see if the right is covered by any of the main human rights conventions. In the case of our example, you will find several pages related to "Women and Marriage," with an overview of the situation followed by brief outlines of basic rights covered by various conventions and other documents.

If, on the other hand, you were looking for information on reproductive rights, or housing, land and property rights for women, you would find these in Section 3: "Developing Rights," the

People cannot participate in things they do not know about.

INTRODUCTION

section that deals with rights not yet recognized in a convention but for which women are actively fighting.

If you have found the right you are looking for in Section 2, you should then turn to Section 5 to determine whether your country is a party to the relevant convention(s) and is therefore bound to guarantee you that right. If your country is a party, i.e. has ratified the specific convention(s), you should then try to find out whether the right has been made a law in your country, whether your country has made any "reservations" to the convention (which means that it doesn't have to guarantee that particular right), whether women's groups and politicians in your country are already actively fighting for that right, and so on.

If the information on the specific right you are searching for is in Section 3: "Developing Rights," you might want to explore ways for women in your community or country to link up with some of the contacts listed, and in that way become part of the global women's movement.

Rights of Women is designed primarily for all individuals, groups and organizations actively working on behalf of women's human rights, but most especially for activists working at the local level. Every effort has been made to make this manual one that is easy-to-use, while still retaining essential legal language and context. As with all materials produced by the International Women's Tribune Centre, it is the result of hard work by many people and many groups, and any feedback received from those who use it would be greatly appreciated.

From the 1998 global campaign postcard produced by the Center for Women's Global Leadership

Understanding Conventions

IN THIS SECTION

Human Rights Conventions...

- Why Are They Important to Women?
- What is a Human Rights Convention?
- How Does a Convention Become Law?
- How Are Conventions Enforced?
- Other Enforcement Procedures?
- UN Institutions that Protect Human Rights?
- Where to Find UN Human Rights Conventions

Human Rights Conventions...

WHY ARE THEY IMPORTANT TO WOMEN?

The campaign for women's human rights has never been stronger. Since the UN Fourth World Conference on Women in Beijing, 1995, 58 countries have adopted legislation or policies to address women's rights. It is true that there are still gross violations of women's basic human rights all over the world, but women's human rights activists are increasingly emerging as a vocal and visible force to be reckoned with.

How has this transformation occurred? The momentum began during the three UN world conferences on women held in Mexico City in 1975, Copenhagen in 1980 and Nairobi in 1985. At these meetings, women of all ethnic, political, professional and economic backgrounds had unparalleled opportunities for networking and coalition building.

The networks and coalitions that were formed did not die when the conference-goers returned home. On the contrary, they became the core of a dynamic global women's movement. By the 1990s, when the UN convened world conferences on the Environment (Rio de Janeiro 1992), Human Rights (Vienna 1993), Population and Development (Cairo 1994), Social Development (Copenhagen 1995), Women (Beijing 1995) and Housing (Istanbul 1996), women were prepared. They participated in these meetings as well-organized, articulate and politically skilled activists.

Significantly, women have taken their successes at these world conferences home. They have capitalized not only on their new skills and new connections, but also on their new confidence in being able to influence policy, to lobby government and to engage in public sector activism. In countries as disparate as India and Venezuela, Uganda and Fiji, women have begun to recognize their own "political clout" and to tap the lessons learned in the international arena to push for change at country level. They have held local tribunals based on the very successful Global Tribunal on Women's Human Rights held at the human rights conference in Vienna. They have organized media campaigns to broadcast the health and reproductive rights

6 RIGHTS OF WOMEN

UNDERSTANDING CONVENTIONS

issues discussed in Cairo. They have transformed the Beijing Platform for Action into a tool for community action.

Now women are going further: they are reaching beyond the policy documents that came out of the global conferences and taking hold of other international agreements—the UN human rights conventions—to press for change. The conventions are the strongest legal tool the UN has to offer. The Convention on the Elimination of All Forms of Discrimination Against Women (CEDAW) is perhaps the best known of these conventions, but it is by no means the only international law that holds promise for women's human rights. To use human rights conventions to fight for women's human rights, women must first understand what they are.

WHAT IS A HUMAN RIGHTS CONVENTION?

A human rights convention defines human rights concepts. It is a legally binding international agreement between states or countries that provides standards of conduct for governments to fulfill. Conventions may also be called treaties, covenants or pacts. By ratifying, or approving, them states agree to ensure that the human rights covered by the convention are enjoyed by everyone in their territories. Many conventions guarantee a wide range of rights, such as the International Covenant on Economic, Social and Cultural Rights, while others address specific rights, such as the Convention on the Nationality of Married Women.

Some international human rights conventions date back to the beginning of this century, when the League of Nations framed a Slavery Convention in 1926. However, the Slavery Convention lacked clarity and neglected to provide machinery for supervising its application.

The majority of human rights conventions therefore—including those that we cover in this book—come from negotiations that have taken place under the auspices of the United Nations. Out of the horrors and tragedies of World War II came a determination by governments to promote human dignity. Thus, in 1948, the fledgling UN proclaimed a Universal Declaration of Human Rights (UDHR), which eloquently describes the "inalienable and inviolable rights of all members of the human family." This declaration marked a moral milestone in the history of the community of nations.

Lacking the force of law, however, its principles had to be transformed into treaties to make them legally binding on countries that ratified them. This resulted in two conventions (called covenants) that distinguished between the different types of human rights: civil and political rights, which countries agreed to protect immediately (the International Covenant on Civil and Political Rights), and economic, social and cultural rights, which countries promised to guarantee over time (the International Covenant on Economic, Social and Cultural Rights). These two con-

A GLOSSARY OF CONVENTION TERMS

Accession
The act whereby a state becomes a party to a treaty already negotiated and signed by other states. It has the same legal force as ratification. Accession usually occurs after the treaty has entered into force.

Adoption
Approval of the final text of a convention by the committee which wrote it. It is then open for signatures, ratification or accession.

Convention
An international agreement among nations. Such agreements may have different names: treaty, covenant, convention or pact.

Covenant
See "Convention".

A GLOSSARY OF CONVENTION TERMS (cont.)

Enter into Force
The treaty becomes a legal document. Agreement is reached on the number of country ratifications needed before a convention is considered enforceable. This number varies, from as few as two (in the case of International Labour Organisation conventions) to as many as 35 (in the case of human rights covenants) and is specified in the final text. The convention "enters into force" after the required number of ratifications has been received.

Protocol
An addition to the original text of a convention. It may include further agreements or it may involve amendments to the original text because of new circumstances. It can be procedural (i.e. it outlines the mechanisms for presenting a claim) or substantive (i.e. it relates to the subject matter of the claim).

UNDERSTANDING CONVENTIONS

ventions, together with the original UDHR, collectively make up what is known as the International Bill of Human Rights.

Subsequent conventions have elaborated on the International Bill of Human Rights by focusing in greater detail on specific human rights areas. For example, while the International Bill of Human Rights covers torture, the Convention Against Torture offers more specific protections.

HOW DOES A CONVENTION BECOME LAW?

When there is a human rights violation or injustice, it may take years of local, regional and national action before that violation is addressed by the UN. The UN may respond by creating a non-enforceable recommendation, or it may create a convention, which is legally binding. When the UN adopts a convention, it presents that convention to all Member States of the UN.

A state can sign the convention, indicating that it intends to follow it, but the convention only becomes legally binding after it has been ratified or approved according to the legal procedures of that state. Unless a country has either ratified or acceded to a human rights convention, it is not legally obligated to ful-

fill any of the responsibilities written in the convention.

Each convention needs to be ratified by a certain number of countries before it enters into force, or becomes law. All the conventions we refer to in this book have entered into force.

The state may sign and ratify the convention at a later date—that is, any time after the convention was first presented—and this process is called accession. The state may also make a reservation at that time. This is a statement that indicates the state does not agree with certain provisions of the convention, and is therefore not legally obligated to

PREAMBLE or INTRODUCTION

ARTICLES or PARAGRAPHS that spell out
• human rights guarantees & protections;
• states' responsibilities;
• mechanisms for monitoring the convention; &
• ratification rules

OPTIONAL PROTOCOLS (additional agreements to the convention)

Reservations, which states make when they disagree with specific parts of the convention.

THE ANATOMY OF A CONVENTION

Note: Not all conventions have optional protocols and some do not allow reservations.

8 RIGHTS OF WOMEN

UNDERSTANDING CONVENTIONS

fulfill those parts of the convention. Reservations must not be incompatible with the overall purpose of the convention, however, and there are some human rights treaties that are not open to reservations because they cover human rights that are considered too fundamental to disagree with. If at any time states decide they no longer agree with the overall intent of a convention, they may denounce or withdraw from it, as long as they give the United Nations advance notice.

Some human rights conventions have optional protocols, or further agreements, added to the main convention. These protocols may increase the human rights protections covered by the convention or set up additional means of enforcement and complaint procedures. States must separately ratify or accede to the protocol before they are obligated to live by its provisions.

To know where your country stands on a particular human rights convention, you must find out whether your country has:

- ✔ ratified or acceded to the convention,
- ✔ made any reservations and withdrawn any reservations,
- ✔ denounced, or withdrawn from, the convention,
- ✔ ratified or acceded to the convention's optional protocols.

HOW ARE CONVENTIONS ENFORCED?

The UN enforces international human rights law in ways that are very different from how states enforce their national laws. There is no international police force for human rights violations and there are no permanent international courts where individuals can place a claim against their government. The International Court of Justice in the Hague hears cases from states but not individuals. A treaty setting up a permanent International Criminal Court was adopted by a vote of 120 countries in Rome in July 1998 but has yet to come into force at the time of this writing.

Instead, the system relies heavily on political pressure to enforce human rights law, and it is states—not individuals—who are responsible for human rights violations. Most countries cooperate with this system because they are very sensitive to political pressure and do not want to be known internationally as a human rights violator. Activists can influence human rights enforcement by learning what the official procedures are for exerting political pressure and how to participate in them. Media pressure can help fuel political pressure, but here we focus on the official methods of enforcement. (For more information on how to use media pressure, see Section 4: A Tribunal: Making Women's Voices Heard.)

There are two main ways to bring up human rights violations within the UN sys-

A GLOSSARY OF CONVENTION TERMS (cont.)

Ratification
The legal act by which a country that has signed the convention agrees to be bound by its provisions; usually ratification requires that the national legislative body agrees to the convention. A certain number of country ratifications are required before a convention comes into force.

Reservation
When a country specifies that it will not accept certain provisions at the time of ratification. Reservations can also refer to which dependent territories are covered or not covered by the provisions. Some conventions have a provision prohibiting reservations.

Signature
Indicates that a country supports the purposes of the document, but is not legally committed to comply with the provisions until the country's legislature officially ratifies it.

A GLOSSARY OF CONVENTION TERMS (cont.)

States parties
The name by which those countries that have ratified or acceded to a convention are known. The terms of the convention are binding only upon states parties.

Succession
Means that a newly formed state has agreed to inherit the treaty obligations of its predecessor.

Treaty
See Convention. A treaty is more likely to cover political relations among countries while conventions deal with human rights, administrative and technical matters.

UNDERSTANDING CONVENTIONS

tem. The first is by following the enforcement and complaint procedures established by each convention. The second is by approaching some of the other UN agencies and offices that focus on human rights. In this section, we look primarily at the convention procedures and only briefly discuss the second way of enforcing human rights; at the end of the section, we list resources for those who need more information about the UN agencies and offices that work for human rights.

The four most common ways of ensuring enforcement of conventions are:

1. It is written into the convention that a committee of experts should be established to monitor the convention.

2. The states that ratify the convention must provide periodic reports to the committee on the ways in which the convention is being implemented within their countries.

3. A state that has ratified the convention may make a complaint to the committee about another state's failure to implement the convention.

4. Under certain circumstances, individuals may make a complaint to the com-

CONVENTIONS WITH ESTABLISHED TREATY BODIES

CONVENTION	TREATY BODY	# OF MEMBERS	ACCEPTS INDIVIDUAL COMPLAINTS
International Covenant on Civil and Political Rights	Human Rights Committee	18 members	Yes
International Covenant on Economic, Social and Cultural Rights	Did not establish a committee itself*	18 members	
Convention on the Elimination of All Forms of Discrimination Against Women	Committee on the Elimination of Discrimination Against Women	23 members	Under discussion
International Convention on the Elimination of All Forms of Racial Discrimination	Committee on the Elimination of Racial Discrimination	18 members	Yes
Convention Against Torture and Other Cruel, Inhuman or Degrading Treatment or Punishment	Committee Against Torture	10 members	Yes
Convention on the Rights of the Child	Committee on the Rights of the Child	10 members	Yes

*The Economic and Social Council (ECOSOC) of the UN filled this gap by setting up the Committee on Economic, Social and Cultural Rights in 1987.

UNDERSTANDING CONVENTIONS

mittee against their own state for violation of rights that are guaranteed by the convention.

The following paragraphs provide details on each of these methods of enforcement.

1. TREATY BODIES

Members of any convention's treaty body must come from a state that has ratified that particular convention. These members do not represent their own states on the body but instead serve individually on the basis of their expertise in human rights.

The treaty body's job is to both help interpret the particular convention and to read and respond to the reports submitted by states that explain how the states are implementing the conventions. Most treaty bodies then submit their own reports either annually or every two years directly to the UN General Assembly. Through this reporting process, states become accountable for their human rights record.

Two of the convention treaty bodies have further power to recommend specific studies or inquiries. The Committee Against Torture can undertake a confidential inquiry, in cooperation with the state concerned, based on reliable information that systematic torture is being practiced by that state. The Committee on the Rights of the Child can also recommend that studies be undertaken on specific issues relating to the rights of the child.

2. STATES' REPORTS

All human rights conventions with treaty bodies require countries that have ratified the convention to submit a report to the treaty body about their progress towards its implementation. States must usually submit their first reports within one year after they have ratified or acceded to the convention, and every two to five years after that, depending on the convention. These state reports describe what legislative, judicial and other practical measures the state has taken to meet its obligations under the convention.

After a state presents its report, the committee may make comments or pose questions to the state and the state may then respond, usually after a specified time period. In this way, a dialogue is created. The whole discussion is summed up in 'Concluding Comments' which identify key issues and recommendations, including areas needing "further improvement" (a euphemism for disturbing trends). The committee has no way of directly forcing a state to act on its recommendations and suggestions, but states usually take into account the committee's views for political reasons.

State reports provide important opportunities for women human rights activists to become involved in the enforcement process. First you must find out when your country is due to make its report and who is responsible for writing it. Contact the secretariat of a committee or the UN High

FACT

State reports provide an opportunity for activists to become involved in the enforcement process.

UNDERSTANDING CONVENTIONS 11

UNDERSTANDING CONVENTIONS

FACT

States generally take remedial action because of political pressure.

Commissioner for Human Rights (to get these addresses, see Section 5: Resource Kit). You could also contact your government's Foreign Affairs department.

Then you might consider any of the following actions:

- Lobby the people responsible for the report for public participation in the writing and research of the report.

- Campaign for the human rights that are guaranteed by the convention but have been inadequately implemented in your country. You can do this both before, during and after the state report has been written. If done before or during, the information raised by your campaign could be included in the state report, giving the committee a fuller picture of human rights in your country.

- Write your own reports and send them directly to members of the committee or to the secretariat of the committee. Find out from the secretariat which approach is best.

- Find out if any women's organizations from your country send representatives to the committee meetings, and work with them to prepare submissions.

- Use the committee's responses or questions as lobbying tools in your own country.

- Inform the media of the report and the committee's response.

3. COMPLAINTS BY STATES

Under some conventions and under very specific circumstances, states may inform the committee of experts that another state is not fulfilling its obligations under the convention. Although this is important to be aware of, this process has seldom, if ever, been utilized and therefore we have not included any details here.

4. COMPLAINTS BY INDIVIDUALS

Three of the human rights conventions permit individuals to make a complaint about human rights violations: the International Convention on the Elimination of Racial Discrimination, the Convention Against Torture and, because of its optional protocol, the International Covenant on Civil and Political Rights. Women around the world are currently working for a similar optional protocol to the Convention on the Elimination of All Forms of Discrimination Against Women (CEDAW) with an aim to having it passed by the year 2000. NGOs and individual activists are involved in this process by canvassing governments.

Individuals must make their complaints about violations in writing. (Your local UN office will provide guidelines for making complaints. See "Where to Find United Nations Human Rights Conventions" on page 15 for how to find regional UN offices.) In order to be admissible, or acceptable, an individual complaint must satisfy certain conditions:

- The complaint must be about a human rights violation that is covered by the

UNDERSTANDING CONVENTIONS

convention and the state involved must have ratified or acceded to the convention or optional protocol.

- The victim of the alleged violation must be under the state's jurisdiction.

- The person making the complaint cannot be anonymous. She must be the victim of the alleged human rights violation or an individual or organization acting on her behalf (specific rules on this vary, depending on the committee).

- All remedies available within the state, usually through the judicial system, must first have been exhausted, unless it can be proven that this would take an unreasonably long time.

- The violation must not be concurrently handled under another international procedure.

If the complaint meets all these conditions and is considered admissible, the committee will examine it and decide whether or not that person's human rights have been violated. The committee then informs both the individual and state involved of its opinion. A committee usually makes specific recommendations about what the state should do to redress the violation, although it cannot force a state to make the necessary changes or reparations. However, states generally do take remedial action because of political pressure. All in all, the individual complaint process may take up to three or four years.

OTHER ENFORCEMENT PROCEDURES

In addition to the human rights enforcement procedures established by the various conventions, the UN has established the following other general methods for making complaints—methods which do not depend on a country having ratified or acceded to a human rights convention.

1. WORKING GROUPS AND SPECIAL RAPPORTEURS

Often at the urging of human rights groups and individual activists, UN commissions will establish different working groups and appoint special rapporteurs to investigate and report on various types of human rights violations. Special rapporteurs are individual experts assigned to work directly with particular countries that have especially urgent human rights situations. They focus on specific issues within the human rights field.

Special rapporteurs and working groups carry out much of the work of a commission by working closely with both governments and NGOs. They gather reports on human rights violations, deal with individual complaints and make recommendations for action. NGOs can aid in the work

FACT

Special rapporteurs are individual experts assigned to work directly with countries that have particularly urgent human rights situations. They focus on specific issues within the human rights field.

RESOURCES

Women's Human Rights Step by Step: A Practical Guide to Using International Human Rights Law and Mechanisms to Defend Women's Human Rights (see page 23 for details).

Women's Passport to Dignity forthcoming December 1998. Features case studies from around the world illustrating how the human rights framework has been used to foster change for women.

People's Decade of Human Rights Education
526 W. 111th St., Suite 4E
New York, NY 10025, USA
Tel: (1-212) 749-3156
Fax: (1-212) 666-6325
E-mail: <pdhre@igc.apc.org>
Web site: <http//www.pdhre.org>

UNDERSTANDING CONVENTIONS

of special rapporteurs and working groups by providing them with information and suggestions that are then presented to the commission. In this way, special rapporteurs or working groups can be an effective medium through which individuals can make a complaint about human rights violations.

2. MAKING PUBLIC AND PRIVATE COMPLAINTS

There are two procedures (known as 1235 and 1503) for making petitions, or complaints, about gross violations of human rights to the UN Commission on Human Rights and its Sub-Commission on the Prevention of Discrimination and Protection of Minorities. States and individuals can make petitions or complaints under either procedure; however, under 1235 all communications relating to the petition are public, whereas under the other procedure (1503) all communications are private. There are specific conditions that must be met to make a petition; contact the Commission for more information.

UN INSTITUTIONS THAT PROTECT HUMAN RIGHTS

1. UN HIGH COMMISSIONER FOR HUMAN RIGHTS

This office was established following the World Conference on Human Rights in Vienna in 1993. The High Commissioner is responsible for coordinating human rights throughout the entire UN system. A broad mandate enables her to be actively involved in addressing almost any violation of human rights in the world.

2. UN COMMISSION ON HUMAN RIGHTS

The Commission is composed of 53 state representatives, and the Office of the High Commissioner for Human Rights operates as its secretariat. The Commission is responsible for coordinating the human rights activities of the UN and is the main UN forum for dealing with human rights violations. NGOs in Consultative Status with the UN and human rights activists who have obtained accreditation for specific meetings can participate as observers.

3. UN SUB-COMMISSION ON PREVENTION OF DISCRIMINATION AND PROTECTION OF MINORITIES

The Sub-Commission is a subsidiary group of the UN Commission on Human Rights. Composed of 26 members who are experts in various human rights fields, the Sub-Commission's role has been interpreted very broadly and includes undertaking studies and making recommendations to the Commission about the prevention of discrimination of any kind relating to human rights. The Sub-Commission has several working groups and special rapporteurs that work specifically on human rights issues.

4. UN COMMISSION ON THE STATUS OF WOMEN

The CSW consists of 45 state representatives and 45 state observers, and the UN Division for the Advancement of Women operates as its secretariat. It meets annually for two weeks in March, and works on reports, studies and recommendations on a wide range of women's human rights

UNDERSTANDING CONVENTIONS

issues. The Convention on the Elimination of All Forms of Discrimination Against Women (CEDAW) came from the CSW. Any accusations of states violating women's human rights are reviewed in confidence by a special Communications Working Group of the Commission (see Other Enforcement Procedures #2, page 14). NGOs in Consultative Status with the UN can participate in meetings of the CSW as observers.

WHERE TO FIND UNITED NATIONS HUMAN RIGHTS CONVENTIONS

UN human rights conventions are free and accessible to everybody, and there are a number of ways to find them. First you must be sure of the exact and complete name of the convention you are looking for (see the ratification charts in Section 5: Resource Kit). The conventions are available in English, French and Spanish, Arabic, Chinese and Russian. Regional UN offices rarely translate conventions into local languages or dialects—unless the convention originated from that particular region. However, sometimes local NGOs work with regional UN offices to translate a convention so that the information reaches more of the people who can make best use of it. If you would like to do this, you should first get written permission from the UN Publications board (see address below).

UN CENTRAL OFFICES

Office of the High Commissioner for Human Rights (UNHCHR)
To obtain copies of human rights conventions, contact:
Focal Point on Human Rights of Women
Office of the UNHCHR
Palais des Nations
1211 Geneva 10, **Switzerland**
Tel: (41-22) 917-3401 or 917-3794
Fax: (41-22) 917-0214

or
UN Office of the UNHCHR
United Nations
New York, NY 10017, **USA**
Tel: (1-212) 963-5930
Fax: (1-212) 963-4097
Web site: <www.unhchr.ch>

Copies of conventions relating specifically to the rights of women can be obtained from:
Division for the Advancement of Women, DC2-1200
United Nations, 2 UN Plaza
New York, NY 10017, **USA**
Tel: (1-212) 963-2264
Fax: (1-212) 963-3463
E-mail: <daw@un.org>
Web site:
<http://www.un.org/dpcsd/daw>

or
UN Publications
DC2-2853, United Nations
New York, NY 10017, **USA**
Tel: (1-212) 963-8302 or (1-800) 253-9646
Fax: (1-212) 963-3489
E-mail: <publications@un.org>
Web site: <www.un.org/publications>

REGIONAL UN OFFICES

The UN Office of Communications and Public Information (UN/OCPI)
operates 70 UN Information Centres worldwide that disseminate global information locally and local information globally.

Conventions and other documents are available from these offices. To find one in your region contact:
UN Office of Communications and Public Information (UN/OCPI)
Public Inquiries Unit
United Nations
New York, NY 10017, **USA**
Tel: (1-212) 963-4475/9246
Fax: (1-212) 963-0071
E-mail: <inquiries@un.org>
Web site:
<www.un.org/moreinfo/pubinq.html>

FACT | UNDERSTANDING CONVENTIONS

The Internet is another way for people who have access to the World Wide Web to find UN conventions. It also offers you the added advantage of being able to download material to use in your own publications.

Even if you yourself do not have access to a computer or to the Internet, you may be able to access information by visiting your local library, college and/or university.

Here are some useful Web sites:

1. ‹http://www.un.org›
This is the general site for all information about the UN. Here you will find news of UN events, documents, general information and more. You can search for whatever information you need by subject, popular name, official title or document number.

2. ‹http://www.un.org/womenwatch›
This is the UN Internet Gateway on the Advancement and Empowerment of Women. Here you will find all official documents of the UN Commission on the Status of Women, UN Global Conferences on Women and more. Under the heading UN Working for Women, you will find copies of the Declaration on the Elimination of Violence Against Women (1993), CEDAW (1979), the draft of the Optional Protocol to CEDAW, and the Declaration on the Protection of Women and Children in Emergencies. Under UN Conference documents you will find the Beijing Platform for Action (1995).

3. ‹http://www.unhchr.ch›
This site for the Office of the UN High Commissioner for Human Rights in Geneva contains the human rights conventions and optional protocols in French and Spanish as well as English. It also has documents from the Commission on Human Rights annual sessions, including all reports of the Special Rapporteur on Violence Against Women.

4. ‹http://www.umn.edu/humanrts/instree/auoe.htm›
This is the site of the Human Rights Library of the University of Minnesota. It contains a collection of documents on women's human rights, including the conventions, in English, French and Spanish.

5. ‹http://www.hurinet.org›
This human rights information service is comprised of multilingual information on all aspects of human rights on an international level. It also provides general UN information, official UN documents and information on international law.

BOOKS

Women and Human Rights: The Basic Documents (1996)
Center for the Study of Human Rights, Columbia University
Presents the principal international human rights agreements and instruments relating to the human rights of women.
Available through:
Women, Ink., 777 UN Plaza, New York, NY 10017, **USA**
Tel: (212) 687-8633
Fax: (212) 661-2704
E-mail: ‹wink@womenink.org›
Web site: ‹http://www.womenink.org›
(see page 148 for ordering information)

Human Rights: A Compilation of International Instruments, 2 volumes,
Office of the UNHCHR, Geneva, 1994.

International Instruments of the UN
Anniversary Issue,
Office of the UNHCHR, Geneva, 1997.

These books, which provide UN human rights instruments, are available from:
United Nations Bookshop/United Nations
New York, NY 10017, **USA**
Tel: (212) 963-7680
Fax: (212) 963-4910
E-mail: ‹bookshop@un.org›
Web site: ‹www.un.org/bookshop›

United Nations Bookshop
Palais de Nations
CH-1211 Geneva 10, **SWITZERLAND**
Tel: (41-22) 917-2614
Fax: (41-22) 917-0027
E-mail: ‹unpubli@unog.ch›

Basic Instruments on Human Rights, 4th ed.,
Ian Brownlie, Clarendon Press, Oxford, 1995.

Form for Documenting Violations of Women's Human Rights

(Sample form prepared using UN Fact Sheet No. 7 Communication Procedures.)

Send to:
Office of the UN High Commissioner for Human Rights,
United Nations, 8-14 avenue de la Paix, 1211 Geneva 10, **Switzerland**

DATE _____

I. INFORMATION CONCERNING THE AUTHOR OF THE COMMUNICATION

Last Name _____ First Name(s) _____

Nationality _____ Profession _____

Date and place of birth _____

Present address _____

_____

Address for exchange of confidential correspondence (if other than present address)

_____

_____

Submitting the communication as (check any of the following that apply to your situation):

❏ (a) Victim(s) of the specific violation(s) set forth below

❏ (b) Representative/legal counsel of the alleged victim(s)

❏ (c) Representative of alleged victim in other capacity

If (c) is checked, author should explain:

(i) In what capacity she or he is acting on behalf of the victim(s), e.g. family relationship or other links with the alleged victim(s)

_____

(ii) Why the victim(s) is (are) unable to submit the communication herself (themselves)

_____

II. INFORMATION CONCERNING ALLEGED VICTIM(S)

Last Name _____ First Name(s) _____

Nationality _____ Profession _____

Date and place of birth _____

Present address _____

_____

Address for confidential correspondence

_____

_____

_____

III. NAME OF STATE, THE ARTICLES VIOLATED, AND POSSIBLE DOMESTIC REMEDIES

Name of the State party (country) and, if relevant, the private perpetrator of the violation, to which the communication is directed:

_____

Steps taken by or on behalf of the alleged victim(s) to exhaust domestic remedies/ recourse to the court or other public authorities, when and with what results (if possible, enclose copies of all relevant judicial or administrative decisions)*.

_____
_____
_____

If domestic remedies have not been exhausted, explain why.*

_____

IV. OTHER INTERNATIONAL PROCEDURES

Has the same matter been submitted for examination under another procedure of international investigation or settlement (e.g. the Inter-American Commission on Human Rights, the European Commission on Human Rights)? If so, when and with what results?*

_____
_____
_____

V. FACTS OF THE CLAIM

Indicate whether this is a "group action" complaint or testimony of a specific individual violation

_____
_____

Detailed description of the facts of the alleged violation or violations (including relevant dates)*

_____
_____
_____
_____
_____
_____

Author's signature_____

*Add as many pages as needed for this description. Send completed form to Office of the UN High Commissioner for Human Rights (see top of form on previous page for address).

2

Know Your Rights

IN THIS SECTION

Women and Human Rights

Your Human Rights and the Laws that Protect Them:

- Women and Education
- Women and Employment
- Women and Marriage
- Women Refugees
- Sexual Exploitation and Trafficking
- Women and Torture

Women and

You have the right to the same political, civil, social and economic rights as men do.

"Women's rights are human rights!" Ever since the 1993 World Conference on Human Rights in Vienna this has become a rallying cry for women around the globe. The words express an irrefutable—and obvious—truth. *Of course* women's rights are human rights: women are humans, and so what applies to humans applies to women.

This truth is not only irrefutable, it has also been affirmed in every major international human rights treaty. From the UN's 1948 proclamation on human rights—the Universal Declaration of Human Rights (UDHR)—to the more recent 1979 Convention on the Elimination of All Forms of Discrimination Against Women (CEDAW), discrimination against women is explicitly prohibited. So why are we still insisting, shouting, demanding: Women's rights are human rights?

The short answer is that despite these meticulously worded international treaties, discrimination against women persists on every level in every corner of the world. We all know the statistics. (We all *live* them!) Women make up half the world's population yet they account for only 5 to 10 percent of formal political leadership positions worldwide. Women contribute up to 70 percent of their local and national economies yet receive less than one-tenth of the world's income. Two-thirds of the world's 960 million illiterate people are women. Violence against women both in and out of the home has reached epidemic proportions. In other words, there is a giant gap between the theoretical legal protections against discrimination and women's everyday realities.

To close that gap, women have been organizing and mobilizing—demanding that leaders start paying attention to women's daily realities. We have been looking at the international laws and

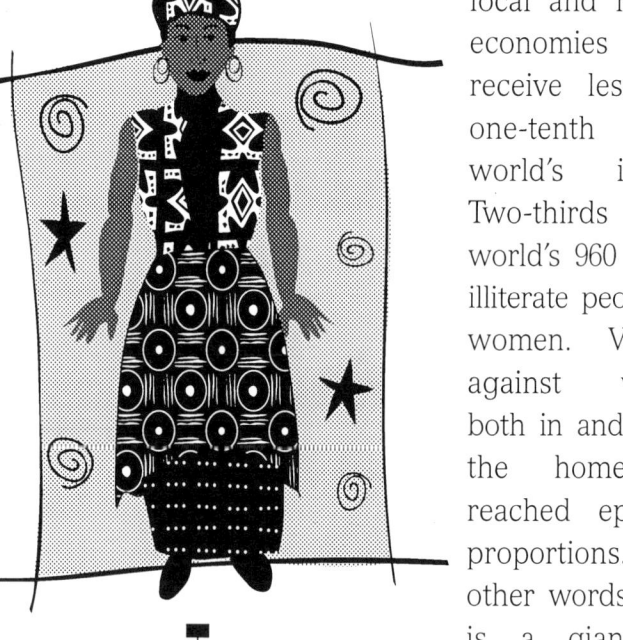

20 RIGHTS OF WOMEN

HUMAN RIGHTS

making sure that they are correctly interpreted and effectively enforced. We have been insisting that the human rights of women are an inalienable, integral and indivisible part of universal human rights. We have been attending UN world conferences (e.g. on women in **Nairobi** in 1985, on children in 1989, on human rights in **Vienna** in 1993, on population in **Cairo** in 1994, on women in **Beijing** in 1995) and holding our own human rights tribunals and hearings. We have been writing our own policy documents, ones that focus on women's private, domestic, as well as public lives. These include the Beijing Platform for Action and the Declaration on the Elimination of Violence Against Women which, although they do not have the force of law (not being conventions), do set a moral standard and can be used for organizing and mobilizing.

We have succeeded in getting the UN to appoint a Special Rapporteur on Violence Against Women—someone whose sole mission is to gather facts and report to the UN on this issue. We have been lobbying for an optional protocol to CEDAW that would enable individuals to bring complaints of violations against states and thus make states far more accountable for discrimination against women. In short, we have been casting a global spotlight on women's human rights.

Women activists have been taking hold of international law and making it their own, and this book is intended as an additional tool for that purpose. Because women have less access to education, and suffer political and economic discrimination, they often have less access to the legal mechanisms that should be at their disposal. So we have analyzed the technical, legal language of these international treaties and paraphrased them in everyday English. (We hope to produce editions in other languages as well.) We have outlined each human right and indicated exactly which part of which law focuses on that right. In doing so, we hope that women will learn what the international conventions say and use them as tools to demand that the countries that have signed and ratified them adopt legislation, establish institutions and promote practices that put into effect the rights recognized in the conventions. Countries are *legally* bound to do this, and we must learn how to compel them to take action.

We start with the human rights that are protected by the UN's basic human rights documents:
• the Universal Declaration on Human Rights (UDHR)

"
In no country do women have political status, access, or influence equal to men's.
"

--Women and Politics Worldwide, p. 30.

FACT

Today women are working to add an optional protocol to CEDAW. This would give individuals the right to complain at the highest international level. about discrimination against women

WOMEN'S HUMAN RIGHTS

You have the right to live safely and to think and express yourself freely, without fear.

- the International Covenant on Civil and Political Rights (ICCPR)

- the International Covenant on Economic, Social and Cultural Rights (ICESCR)

- the International Convention on the Elimination of All Forms of Racial Discrimination (ICERD)

- the Convention Against Torture (CAT)

- the Convention on the Rights of the Child (CRC)

and, without doubt the most important UN document for women,

- the Convention on the Elimination of All Forms of Discrimination Against Women (CEDAW).

CEDAW goes further than the other documents in describing women's human rights. It gives a wider definition of discrimination and discusses women's inequality in the broader context of poverty, racism, armed conflict and development. CEDAW also covers discrimination in the home a critical step in incorporating the domestic realm within the human rights framework.

Finally, the UN Fourth World Conference on Women Platform for Action (PFA) and the Declaration on the Elimination of Violence Against Women (DEVAW) are also included. These are documents that are not legally enforceable—although the CEDAW treaty body has stated that DEVAW is an elaboration of the convention—but they are crucial nonetheless to any discussion on women's human rights. Both strongly

WOMEN'S HUMAN RIGHTS

challenge the premise that women should ever suffer gender discrimination in the name of culture, tradition, religion or for any other reason, and both show the close connections between women's poverty and all forms of discrimination.

On the following pages you will find each human right described. Underneath each right are abbreviations referring to the different conventions or policies that focus on that particular right. (A key to the abbreviations used is found in the margins under the heading "Relevant Conventions.") Since legal documents contain numbered paragraphs, we've included the numbers of the significant paragraphs.

In the international community, these conventions are considered the most important human rights documents. For certain issues, however, human rights violations have been so pervasive that additional, more detailed conventions have been required. You will find some of these set out on the pages that follow the descriptions of the basic rights. By learning which rights are protected in these conventions and how to use them, we can begin to become champions of our own human rights.

SELECTED PUBLICATIONS
AVAILABLE FROM WOMEN, INK.*

Advocacy Kit on CEDAW
Five booklets and nine information sheets on the provisions of CEDAW and its relevance to women's human rights.
UNIFEM/UNICEF, 1995. $5.95

Claiming Our Place: Working the Human Rights System to Women's Advantage
Margaret A. Schuler (Ed.)
Analyses human rights law and examines the conflict between women's human rights and national, cultural and religious particularities.
Women, Law and Development International, 1993. $10.00

Gender Justice: Women's Rights Are Human Rights *Elizabeth Fisher and Linda Gray MacKay*
Uses the Beijing Platform for Action to structure a workshop series intended to educate and inspire action on women's human rights.
Unitarian Universalist Service Committee, 1997. $15.00

Human Rights of Women: National and International Perspectives *Rebecca J. Cook (Ed.)*
Combines reports and case studies with scholarly assessments of international human rights law and its application to women in different cultures.
University of Pennsylvania Press, 1994. $22.95

Local Action/Global Change: Learning About the Human Rights of Women and Girls *Julie Mertus with Malika Dutt and Nancy Flowers*
Uses an "interactive" format to combine the development of rights awareness with issue-oriented activities.
Center for Women's Global Leadershp/UNIFEM, 1998. *(price not yet set)*

Women's Human Rights Step by Step: A Practical Guide for Using International Human Rights Law and Mechanisms to Defend Women's Human Rights
Describes in simple language the concept and content of human rights law, and provides adaptable tools for different legal and political contexts.
Women, Law and Development International/ Women's Rights Project, 1997. $27.50

* Contact information on page 146.

The human rights of women are an inalienable, integral and indivisible part of universal human rights.

WOMEN'S HUMAN RIGHTS

Your HUMAN RIGHTS and the

RELEVANT CONVENTIONS

Universal Declaration of Human Rights
(UDHR)
International Covenant on Civil and Political Rights
(ICCPR)
International Covenant on Economic, Social and Cultural Rights
(ICESCR)
International Convention on the Elimination of All Forms of Racial Discrimination
(ICERD)
Convention Against Torture and Other Cruel, Inhuman or Degrading Treatment or Punishment
(CAT)
Convention on the Rights of the Child
(CRC)
Convention on the Elimination of All Forms of Discrimination Against Women
(CEDAW)

OTHER DOCUMENTS

Declaration on the Elimination of Violence Against Women
(DEVAW)
UN Fourth World Conference on Women Platform for Action
(PFA)

Numbers refer to paragraphs in the conventions. To find these conventions see "Where to Find Conventions" in Section 1.

YOUR POLITICAL AND CIVIL RIGHTS

...freedom, equality and physical integrity

- You have the same human rights and freedoms as everyone else in the world. These rights are inherent in being a human being. They cannot be taken away from you. Everybody, no matter who we are or where we live, should be treated with equal dignity.
  UDHR 1

- You should not be treated differently, or have your rights denied, because of your race, colour, sex, language, religion, political or other opinion, national or social origin, property, birth or other status.
  UDHR 2 • ICCPR 2: 1 • ICESCR 2: 2 • CRC 2
  PFA 232

- You have the right to live without discrimination of any kind based on sex.
  ICCPR 3 •ICESCR 3 • CEDAW 1, 2, 3
  PFA 214, 232 • DEVAW 3e

- You have the right to live without discrimination of any kind based on race.
  ICERD 1, 2, 3 • DEVAW 3e

- All peoples have the right to self-determination. That means colonized or dominated peoples are free to choose their political status and to pursue their own economic, social and cultural development.
  ICCPR 1 • ICESCR 1 • PFA 145a

- Everyone has the right to life, liberty and security of person.
  UDHR 2 • ICCPR 2: 1 • ICESCR 2: 2 • CRC 2
  DEVAW 3a, c

- No one has the right to enslave anyone else. Slavery is a crime.
  UDHR 4 • ICCPR 8

- Women and children have the right to protection from all forms of traffic for the purposes of prostitution or any other forms of exploitation.
  CEDAW 6 • CRC 35, 36
  PFA 230n • DEVAW 2b
  See also "Sexual Exploitation and Trafficking," page 46.

- You have the right to live without suffering, torture or any form of cruel, inhuman or degrading treatment or punishment.
  UDHR 5 • ICCPR 7 • CRC 37 • CAT 12 • DEVAW 3h
  See also "Women and Torture," page 52.

...legal equality

- You have the right to be recognized as a person before the law.
  UDHR 6 • ICCPR 16 • CEDAW 15: 2, 3

- You have the right to be treated by the law in the same way as everyone else, and to be protected by the law without discrimination.
  UDHR 7 • ICCPR 14: 1, 26 • CEDAW 2c, 15: 1 • ICERD 5a
  PFA 232 • DEVAW 3d

24 RIGHTS OF WOMEN

WOMEN'S HUMAN RIGHTS
LAWS that Protect Them

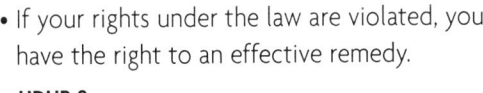

- If your rights under the law are violated, you have the right to an effective remedy.
  UDHR 8

- You may not be arrested or held without good reason. You have the right to challenge your detention in a court of law.
  UDHR 9 • ICCPR 9 • CRC 37d

- If you suffer from any kind of racial discrimination, you have the right to seek justice.
  ICERD 6

- If charged with a crime, you have the right to be presumed innocent until proven guilty.
  UDHR 11: 1 • ICCPR 14: 2 • CRC 40: 2b

- If charged with a crime, you have the right to a fair and public hearing by an independent and impartial tribunal.
  UDHR 10 • ICCPR 14: 1 • CRC 40: 2b

- You cannot be found guilty of a crime that was not a crime when the act was committed.
  UDHR 11: 2 • ICCPR 15 • CRC 40: 2a

- If you are detained, you have the right to be treated with dignity.
  ICCPR 10 • CRC 37c

- In countries that have not abolished the death penalty, it can only be used for the most serious crimes, and those sentenced to death have the right to seek a pardon. Children under 18 and pregnant women shall not receive the death penalty.
  ICCPR 6: 2, 6: 4, 6: 5 • CRC 37a
  See further, Second Optional Protocol to the ICCPR Aiming at the Abolition of the Death Penalty, 1989. *To find this protocol see "Where to Find Conventions" in Section 1.*

- No one shall imprison you for failing to fulfil a contract.
  ICCPR 11

- A foreigner unlawfully present in another country shall not be expelled from that country without a fair process, except where compelling reasons of national security exist.
  ICCPR 13

. . . nationality, freedom of movement and other civil and political rights

- You have the right to a name and a nationality at birth. You have the right to change your nationality, and marriage shall not affect your nationality.
  UDHR 15: 1 • ICCPR 24 • CEDAW 9 • ICERD 5d, iii CRC 7

- No one has the right to intrude in your private or family life without good reason, or to attack your good name.
  UDHR 12 • ICCPR 17 • CRC 16

- You have the right to move freely within the borders of your country. You can also leave and return to any country, including your own.
  UDHR 13 • ICCPR 12 • ICERD 5d, i, ii

- You have the right to seek asylum from persecution in other countries.
  UDHR 14 • CAT 3 • ICCPR 13 • PFA 147, 148
  For more information on the rights of refugees, see "Women and Refugees," page 42.

- You have the right to be treated as a citizen of your country. No one can take away your citizenship or prevent you from changing your country without good reason. Marriage shall not affect your nationality.
  UDHR 15 • CEDAW 9 • ICERD 5d, iii

RELEVANT CONVENTIONS

Universal Declaration of Human Rights
(UDHR)

International Covenant on Civil and Political Rights
(ICCPR)

International Covenant on Economic, Social and Cultural Rights
(ICESCR)

International Convention on the Elimination of All Forms of Racial Discrimination
(ICERD)

Convention Against Torture and Other Cruel, Inhuman or Degrading Treatment or Punishment
(CAT)

Convention on the Rights of the Child
(CRC)

Convention on the Elimination of All Forms of Discrimination Against Women
(CEDAW)

OTHER DOCUMENTS

Declaration on the Elimination of Violence Against Women
(DEVAW)

UN Fourth World Conference on Women Platform for Action
(PFA)

Numbers refer to paragraphs in the conventions. To find these conventions see "Where to Find Conventions" in Section 1.

BASIC RIGHTS OF WOMEN **25**

RELEVANT CONVENTIONS

Universal Declaration of Human Rights
(UDHR)

International Covenant on Civil and Political Rights
(ICCPR)

International Covenant on Economic, Social and Cultural Rights
(ICESCR)

International Convention on the Elimination of All Forms of Racial Discrimination
(ICERD)

Convention Against Torture and Other Cruel, Inhuman or Degrading Treatment or Punishment
(CAT)

Convention on the Rights of the Child
(CRC)

Convention on the Elimination of All Forms of Discrimination Against Women
(CEDAW)

OTHER DOCUMENTS

Declaration on the Elimination of Violence Against Women
(DEVAW)

UN Fourth World Conference on Women Platform for Action
(PFA)

Numbers refer to paragraphs in the conventions. To find these conventions see "Where to Find Conventions" in Section 1.

WOMEN'S HUMAN RIGHTS

- You have the right to freedom of thought, conscience and religion.

  UDHR 18 • ICCPR 18 • ICERD 5d, vii • CRC 14

- You have the right to freely express your opinion without fear of punishment, both within your country and to people in other countries.

  UDHR 19 • ICCPR 19 • ICERD 5d, viii • CRC 12, 13, 17

- War propaganda shall be against the law. Any advocacy of national, racial or religious hatred that promotes discrimination, hostility or violence shall be prohibited by the law.

  ICCPR 20

- You have the right to gather peacefully and associate with others in public or private. No one may force you to join any group if you do not wish to.

  UDHR 20 • ICCPR 21, 22 • ICERD 5d, ix • CRC 15
  PFA 190c

- You have the right to take part in the government of your country, to vote and to have equal access to public services.

  UDHR 21 • ICCPR 25 • CEDAW 7 • ICERD 5c
  PFA 190, 191, 192, 195

- You have the right to represent your government and participate in international organizations.

  CEDAW 8 • PFA 190, 191, 193, 195

- Human beings have the right to live in the kind of world where their rights and freedoms are respected.

  UDHR 28 • PFA 210-216, 221-223, 279c

- You have the right to be free from all forms of apartheid, racism, colonialism, violence and foreign occupation that prevent you from enjoying your full rights.

  ICERD 3
  CEDAW preamble • PFA 214, 216, 224-226, 232

- Our human rights can be limited only by law and then only to protect other people's rights, meet society's sense of right and wrong, maintain order and look after the welfare of democratic society as a whole. We all have a responsibility to the people around us and we can only develop fully as individuals by taking care of each other.

  UDHR 29

YOUR ECONOMIC, SOCIAL AND CULTURAL RIGHTS

- Everyone is entitled to economic, social and cultural rights that allow them dignity and freedom to develop as individuals.

  UDHR 22 • CEDAW 11: 1e • ICERD 5e • CRC 27
  PFA 220

- You have the right to an adequate standard of living for yourself and your family, including food, clothing, housing and medical care.

  ICESCR 11 • CEDAW 14h • ICERD 5e, iii • CRC 27: 1
  PFA 58

- Parents have the primary responsibility to ensure that their child has an adequate standard of living and states have a duty to assist those responsible to implement this right.

  CRC 27: 2, 3

- Everyone has the right to social security.

  UDHR 22 • ICESCR 9 • CEDAW 11: 1e, 14c, 13a
  ICERD 5e, iv • CRC 26 • PFA 580

26 RIGHTS OF WOMEN

WOMEN'S HUMAN RIGHTS

- Everyone has the right to social services and security in the event of sickness, old age or other circumstances, including child-care for working parents.
  UDHR 25 • CEDAW 11: 2c • ICERD 5e, iv • CRC 18: 2, 3
  PFA 58o

- Rural women have the same rights as other women and men.
  CEDAW 14 • PFA 58n, 62a

. . . employment rights

- You have the right to work and to freely choose your job.
  UDHR 23: 1 • ICESCR 6 • CEDAW 11a • ICERD 5e, i

- You have the right to work in fair and safe conditions and to be paid enough for an adequate standard of living, supplemented by social protections if necessary. Women have the right to the same working conditions as men, especially equal pay for equal work or work of equal value.
  **UDHR 23: 2, 3 • ICESCR 7a, b • CEDAW 11, 14: 2e
  ICERD 5e: i** • PFA 165a, b • DEVAW 3g

- You have the right to form or join trade unions.
  UDHR 23: 4 • ICCPR 22 • ICESCR 8 • ICERD 5e, ii
  PFA 165r, 178h, i, 190c

- You have the right to rest and leisure. You do not have to work unreasonable hours and you have the right to holidays with pay.
  UDHR 24 • ICESCR 7d • CRC 31 • PFA 180a

- You cannot be dismissed from your employment because of pregnancy, while on maternity leave or because of your marital status.
  CEDAW 11: 2a • PFA 165c

- You have the right to maternity leave with pay or to adequate social security benefits without loss of former employment, seniority or social allowances.
  ICESCR 10: 2 • CEDAW 11: 2b • PFA 165a

- You are entitled to special protection at work if you are pregnant.
  CEDAW 11: 2d

- Children have the right to special protections from economic exploitation including a minimum age for employment.
  ICESCR 10: 3 • CRC 32 • PFA 166l, 178m, n
  See also "Women and Employment," page 33.

. . . housing

- You have the right to adequate housing.
  UDHR 25:1 • ICESCR 11:1 • CEDAW 14:2h

. . . property and credit

- You have the right to own goods, land and other property.
  UDHR 17 • CEDAW 16:1h • ICERD 5d, v

- You have the right to bank loans, mortgages and other forms of financial credit.
  CEDAW 13b • PFA 62, 165e, j, 166a, d

- As a rural woman, you have the right to agricultural credit and loans, marketing facilities, appropriate technology and equal treatment in land and agrarian reform.
  CEDAW 14: 2g • PFA 61b, 62, 166c

. . . health

- You have the right to the highest attainable level of physical and mental health and the right to equal access to health services, including family planning.
  ICESCR 12 • CEDAW 12 • CRC 24
  PFA 89, 106b • DEVAW 3f

- You have the right to special health services with respect to pregnancy, childbirth and the postnatal period.
  ICESCR 12: 2a • CEDAW 12: 2 • CRC 24: 1d, f
  PFA 106e

RELEVANT CONVENTIONS

Universal Declaration of Human Rights
(UDHR)

International Covenant on Civil and Political Rights
(ICCPR)

International Covenant on Economic, Social and Cultural Rights
(ICESCR)

International Convention on the Elimination of All Forms of Racial Discrimination
(ICERD)

Convention Against Torture and Other Cruel, Inhuman or Degrading Treatment or Punishment
(CAT)

Convention on the Rights of the Child
(CRC)

Convention on the Elimination of All Forms of Discrimination Against Women
(CEDAW)

OTHER DOCUMENTS

Declaration on the Elimination of Violence Against Women
(DEVAW)

UN Fourth World Conference on Women Platform for Action
(PFA)

*Numbers refer to paragraphs in the conventions.
To find these conventions see "Where to Find Conventions" in Section 1.*

BASIC RIGHTS OF WOMEN

RELEVANT CONVENTIONS

Universal Declaration of Human Rights **(UDHR)**

International Covenant on Civil and Political Rights **(ICCPR)**

International Covenant on Economic, Social and Cultural Rights **(ICESCR)**

International Convention on the Elimination of All Forms of Racial Discrimination **(ICERD)**

Convention Against Torture and Other Cruel, Inhuman or Degrading Treatment or Punishment **(CAT)**

Convention on the Rights of the Child **(CRC)**

Convention on the Elimination of All Forms of Discrimination Against Women **(CEDAW)**

OTHER DOCUMENTS

Declaration on the Elimination of Violence Against Women **(DEVAW)**

UN Fourth World Conference on Women Platform for Action **(PFA)**

Numbers refer to paragraphs in the conventions. To find these conventions see "Where to Find Conventions" in Section 1.

WOMEN'S HUMAN RIGHTS

... education

- You have the right to an education. Elementary education shall be free and compulsory, secondary education shall be accessible to all, higher education shall be equally accessible to all on the basis of merit.

  UDHR 26 • ICESCR 13 and 14 • CEDAW 10 • ICERD 5e, v • CRC 28 • PFA 80, 81, 279a

- Women and girls have the same rights to all forms of education as men and boys.

  CEDAW 10 • CRC 28
  PFA 80, 81, 82, 87a, b

- You have a continuing right to education and training throughout your life.

  CEDAW 10e, f • PFA 82, 88

- The content of education must include development of respect for human rights and must promote understanding, tolerance and friendship among all groups and individuals.

  UDHR 26: 2 • ICESCR 13: 1 • CRC 29
  PFA 233g, 279c

- Any stereotyped concept of the roles of women and men must be eliminated through education.

  CEDAW 10c • PFA 83a, b, c, 236, 243 a, d, e

  See also "Women and Education," page 30.

... culture

- You have the right to participate freely in the cultural life of the community and to enjoy the arts and all the benefits of scientific progress.

  UDHR 27 • ICESCR 15 • CEDAW 13c • ICERD 5e, vi CRC 31 • PFA 75, 85b, 231a, 239g, d

- Ethnic, religious, linguistic or indigenous minorities have the right to enjoy their own culture, to practice their own religion and to use their own language.

  ICCPR 27 • CRC 30 • PFA 232a, o, 242d

- You have the right to go into any place and use any service that is used by the general public, including hotels, restaurants, cafes, theatres and parks, without distinction as to race, colour, or national or ethnic origin.

  ICERD 5e, f

YOUR RIGHTS CONCERNING MARRIAGE AND FAMILY

- You have the right to marry, and both partners have equal rights in their marriage, in their family responsibilities, and at the dissolution of marriage. Both women and men must give their free and full agreement to marriage. The family is entitled to protection by the state.

  UDHR 16 • ICCPR 23 • ICESCR 10: 1 • CEDAW 16: 1a, b, c ICERD 5d, iv • PFA 274e, 277a

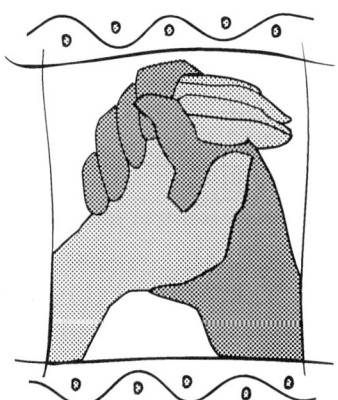

- You have the same right as your spouse to family planning services.

  CEDAW 12: 1, 14: 2b, 16: 1e • PFA 94, 95, 106e

- You have the same rights as your spouse in all matters relating to your children.

  CEDAW 16: 1d, e, f • CRC 18.

- You have the same rights as your spouse to choose a family name, a profession and an occupation.

  CEDAW 16: 1g

RIGHTS OF WOMEN

WOMEN'S HUMAN RIGHTS

- You can acquire, change or retain your nationality and your children's nationality regardless of your husband's nationality. You have the same rights as a man with respect to the nationality of your children.
  CEDAW 9: 1 and 9: 2
  See also "Women and Marriage," page 38.

...additional protections for children

- Every child has the right to special protections without discrimination, including discrimination because of what her/his parents or guardians do or believe.
  ICCPR 24 • CRC 2: 2 • PFA 259, 274f, 276b, d

- In any situation, the best interests of a child shall be a primary consideration. At the same time, parents' rights and responsibilities must also be taken into account.
  CRC 3 • PFA 267

- Children have the right to live with their parent(s) unless separation is in the best interests of the child. In the case of separation from one or both parents, children have the right to maintain personal relations and direct contact with their parents.
  CRC 9

- Children and their parents have the right to apply to enter or leave any country for the purpose of reunification. If children reside in a different state than their parent(s), they have the right to maintain personal relationships.
  CRC 10

- Countries must prevent and remedy kidnapping or the keeping of children abroad.
  CRC 11

- Countries must ensure that children have access to information from a variety of sources and that the mass media distributes information that is socially and culturally beneficial.
  CRC 17 • PFA 239g, 242d

- Children are entitled to special protections when they do not have parents or are separated from their family, taking into account each child's cultural background.
  CRC 20

- Refugee children are entitled to special protections.
  CRC 22 • PFA 147b

- If adoption is permitted in a country, it must be carried out with the best interest of the child as the primary consideration.
  CRC 21

- Children with disabilities have rights to special care, education and training to help them enjoy a full and decent life.
  CRC 23 • PFA 280c

- Children have the right to protection from the illicit use of narcotic drugs and from participation in the production of such drugs.
  CRC 33 • PFA 282a

- Children have the right to be protected from sexual exploitation and abuse, including unlawful sexual activity, prostitution and pornography.
  CRC 34 • PFA 230m, 283b, d

- Children under 15 have the right not to be recruited into armed forces or to have any direct part in armed conflict.
  CRC 38: 1, 2, 3

- Child victims of armed conflict, torture or maltreatment have the right to treatment that promotes physical and psychological recovery and social reintegration.
  CRC 39 • CAT 12

- Children in conflict with the law have the right to treatment that promotes each child's sense of dignity. Children have the right to basic guarantees as well as legal assistance for their defence.
  CRC 40

RELEVANT CONVENTIONS

Universal Declaration of Human Rights
(UDHR)

International Covenant on Civil and Political Rights
(ICCPR)

International Covenant on Economic, Social and Cultural Rights
(ICESCR)

International Convention on the Elimination of All Forms of Racial Discrimination
(ICERD)

Convention Against Torture and Other Cruel, Inhuman or Degrading Treatment or Punishment
(CAT)

Convention on the Rights of the Child
(CRC)

Convention on the Elimination of All Forms of Discrimination Against Women
(CEDAW)

OTHER DOCUMENTS

Declaration on the Elimination of Violence Against Women
(DEVAW)

UN Fourth World Conference on Women Platform for Action
(PFA)

Numbers refer to paragraphs in the conventions. To find these conventions see "Where to Find Conventions" in Section 1.

BASIC RIGHTS OF WOMEN

Women and

You have the right to learn and to use and share your knowledge.

The good news: Adult literacy has made significant strides in the last two decades. Between 1970 and 1992 the literacy rate among developing countries increased from 46 to 69 percent.

The bad news: Fifty years have passed since the Universal Declaration of Human Rights stated that everyone has the right to education. But today nearly 1 billion people worldwide— a fifth of humanity—can neither read nor write, and two-thirds of them are women.

Why do so many women and girls remain unable to read and write? One reason is that, in many places, parents still prefer to send sons rather than daughters to school because women and girls are expected to run households, take care of children and add to the family income. With so many responsibilities, they have little time to learn to read, take vocational classes or build on their own knowledge. Even when women and girls are able to attend school or training workshops, the teaching materials often focus on what boys can do rather than what girls can do. This leads girls to believe that they can't do the same things boys can, and it puts limitations on their imagination.

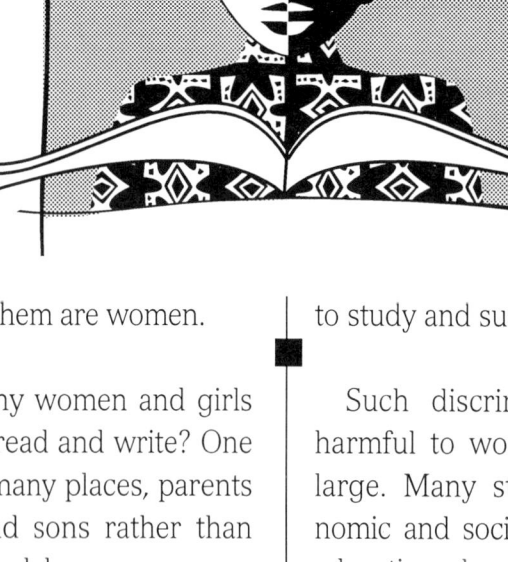

As a result, girls and women attend school for fewer years than boys and men, they do not have as many choices in what they are able to study, and they also receive less encouragement to study and succeed.

Such discrimination is not only harmful to women but to society at large. Many studies prove the economic and social benefits of women's education, showing clearly that it:
- enhances women's (and hence the country's) productivity;
- increases women's employment opportunities and their earning potential;
- reduces infant and child mortality;
- increases life expectancy for the

EDUCATION

whole family;
- reduces fertility rates;
- reduces maternal mortality rates;
- improves health for the whole family; and
- enables women to efficiently manage natural resources.

With education, women feel less isolated and their self-confidence improves, enabling them to contribute more fully to their families and societies. Educating girls increases the likelihood that, when they grow up and marry, their children—particularly their daughters—will enroll and stay in school. It is thus a critical factor in breaking the vicious multigenerational cycle of poor health, low educational opportunity, low income, low self-esteem, high fertility rates and poor overall child health.

How can women ensure that they receive the education that is their right? The first step is to know what their educational rights are. On the following page, you will find the conventions and declarations that help safeguard women's rights to learn.

SELECTED PUBLICATIONS
AVAILABLE FROM WOMEN, INK.*

Gender in Popular Education: Methods for Empowerment *Shirley Walters and Linzi Manicom (Eds.)*
Critical reflections on feminist adult education work in grassroots and community organizations, development projects, and formal institutions.
ZED Books/CACE Publications, 1996. $25.00

Globalization, Adult Education and Training *Shirley Walters (Ed.)*
Looks at the impact of globalization on adult education and training, with a particular focus on women.
ZED Books, 1997. $25.00

Women and Literacy *Marcella Ballara*
Shows how projects to promote women's literacy can contribute to their improved status, better health care and effective economic activity.
ZED Books, 1992. $15.95

Women and the University Curriculum: Towards Equality, Democracy and Peace *Mary Louise Kearney and Anne Holden Rønning (Eds.)*
Examines the links between the university curriculum and gender issues and emphasizes the importance of education as a means of empowering women.
UNESCO, 1996. $32.00

* Contact information on page 146.

FACT

There are 960 million adults in the world who have never had the opportunity to go to school. Two-thirds of them are women.

FACT

Educate a man and you educate an individual; educate a woman and you educate a family.

EDUCATION

Your RIGHTS and the LAWS that Protect Them

RELEVANT CONVENTIONS

Universal Declaration of Human Rights
(UDHR)

International Covenant on Economic, Social and Cultural Rights
(ICESCR)

Convention on the Elimination of All Forms of Discrimination Against Women
(CEDAW)

International Convention on the Elimination of All Forms of Racial Discrimination
(ICERD)

Convention on the Rights of the Child
(CRC)

Convention Against Discrimination in Education
(CDE)

OTHER DOCUMENTS

UN Fourth World Conference on Women Platform for Action
(PFA)

Numbers refer to paragraphs in the conventions. To find these conventions see "Where to Find Conventions" in Section 1.

ACCESS TO BASIC EDUCATION

- You have the right to the same level and standard of education as men and boys.
  UDHR 26: 1 • CEDAW 10 • ICERD 5dv • CDE 1a
  PFA 80a, b, c, d, 87a, b

- You have the right to a free and compulsory primary education.
  UDHR 26: 1 • ICESCR 13: 2a • CEDAW 10 • CRC 28: 1a CDE 4a • PFA 80b, 81b, 279a

- You have the right to accessible secondary education.
  UDHR 26: 1 • CEDAW 10a • ICESCR 13: 2b • CRC 28: 1b CDE 4a • PFA 80b

- You have the right to higher education that is based on merit.
  UDHR 26 • CEDAW 10d • ICESCR 13: 2c • CRC 28: 1c CDE 4a • PFA 80e

- You have the right to education no matter where you live or where you are from.
  CDE 3

- Education shall be directed towards the full development of the human being and an increasing respect for human rights.
  UDHR 26: 2 • ICESCR 13: 1 • CRC 29: 1b • CDE 5: 1a PFA 83j

- Parents may choose alternative schools for their children as long as these schools meet national educational standards.
  UDHR 26: 3 • ICESCR 13: 3 • CDE 5b

- Those who belong to minority groups may carry on their own educational activities, as long as participation is optional.
  CDE 5: c, i-iii • PFA 83v

ACCESS TO OTHER TYPES OF EDUCATION AND TRAINING

- You have the right to vocational training and technology education.
  CEDAW 10a • PFA 82e, 83f

- You have the right to continuing education, literacy programmes and any type of education that reduces the gap in education between men and women.
  CEDAW 10e, f • PFA 82, 88a, b, c

- You have the right to participate in sports and physical education.
  CEDAW 10g

- You have the right to specific educational information to help ensure the health and well-being of families, including information on family planning.
  CEDAW 10h • PFA 83l

- You have the right to the same teacher training as men and boys.
  CEDAW 10a • CDE 4d • PFA 83d, 279f

TEACHING MATERIALS

- All teaching materials should be free of gender stereotypes.
  CEDAW 10c • PFA 83a, b, c, 243a, 276c, 277b

RIGHTS OF WOMEN

Women and EMPLOYMENT

Ask almost any woman worker in the paid workforce if she thinks she is treated fairly and you will get in response a resounding "No!" For even with the great strides women have made in the workplace, they are discriminated against on every level. As a result, women are still: 1) paid less; 2) promoted less; and 3) protected less than men.

Women in the paid workforce will also tell you that much of their day is devoted to labour that remains unrecognized and/or unpaid: making family meals; caring for children; tending livestock; looking after the elderly; and supplementing their family's income with "informal" jobs such as selling vegetables on the roadside or sewing garments at home. Indeed, women's household hours, if calculated, would add an estimated one-quarter to one-third to the world's gross national product.

First, a look at women's earnings. There is still no country in the world where women's average earnings are equal to men's, although the size of this wage gap varies enormously. Among the fifty or so countries reporting non-agricultural wages for women and men, the average wage for women is about 75 percent that of men's. In only four countries—Tanzania, Vietnam, Australia and Sri Lanka—do women earn 90 percent or more of men's wages, and in five—China, South Korea, Japan, Bangladesh and Russia—the proportion is less than 60 percent. Wage-earning mothers are especially disadvantaged. A lack of adequate childcare can force them to take lower-paying jobs, often part-time, and temporary or seasonal work that does not provide benefits.

Second is the problem of promotion. Across all sectors of the economy, women occupy low- or mid-level positions and rarely rise to the top. They are greatly underrepresented in

You have the right to work and to be paid fairly for your work.

EMPLOYMENT

> *If women were paid for all they do there'd be a lot of wages due.*
>
> — Written on a moneybox, made in the shape of a rolling pin, England, 1940s.

FACT

The International Labour Organisation (ILO)—which pre-dates the UN—has a tripartite structure which allows governments, employers and workers to agree on the basic rules for the world of work.

administrative and managerial positions, whether as chief executives or corporate managers, or as legislators, heads of villages and more. Worldwide, women occupy only about 14 percent of these positions. Even in women-dominated professions, such as teaching, women tend to fill the less prestigious, lower-paying preschool and primary school jobs. In secondary schools the percentage of women teachers dramatically decreases, and at the university level nearly all of the higher-paid tenured positions are occupied by men. Part of the problem is that cultural attitudes still view women as nurturers and not as wage-earners, and that often women do not receive the training and thus do not develop the skills that would enable them to advance to more responsible positions. But there is also a consistent pattern of gender discrimination that has to be recognized.

Lastly is the issue of protection—which includes not only safe and fair working conditions, but also job security and health benefits. Overall, protection for women wage earners has worsened due to shifts in the global economy in the 1980s and 1990s. One of those shifts has been a worldwide decrease in the number of public sector jobs, which typically have offered the highest protection for workers in the paid workforce, and at the same time an increase of positions in private industry where protection is often at the mercy of the employers. The manufacturing sector in particular has witnessed a tremendous boom due to the "global assembly line"—factories set up where the labour is cheapest—and the establishment of free trade zones. In 1995, there were free trade zones in 60 countries. Between 1981 and 1991 the number of such zones surged from 80 to 900.

While the increase in work generated by free trade zones means new employment opportunities for many women—particularly young women—the working conditions can range from unhealthy to downright dangerous, and any attempts to fight exploitation or to organize for better benefits or higher wages can lead to the company pulling out and looking for work situations that are more profitable for them. In some countries, including Bangladesh, Vietnam, Indonesia, Morocco, Mexico and Honduras, women and girls may be kept working all night in garment factories and sweatshops so that

EMPLOYMENT

employers can meet the targets and deadlines set by European, Australian and North American retail outlets. In the Philippines, fences and armed guards surround export processing zones. Women doing home-based work for these manufacturers are hidden from the public eye which means that poor working conditions and violations are even more difficult to monitor and eradicate.

Sexual harassment is another area where women workers remain largely unprotected. In Tanzania, for example, a recent survey reports that as many as 90 percent of 200 working women interviewed said that sexual harassment threatened their jobs and economic survival. In the United States, a 1995 survey of 3,000 women found 76 percent reporting some degree of sexual harassment at the workplace.

The UN's main human rights conventions offer only limited protections for workers. The conventions of the International Labour Organisation (a specialized UN agency whose sole focus is on labour issues) do far more. The key conventions concerning women are included on the following pages, such as the ILO's latest treaty, the "Home Work Convention," which came out of a global campaign for home workers rights. Adopted by the General Assembly in 1991, it is now awaiting ratification by Member States.

SELECTED PUBLICATIONS
AVAILABLE FROM WOMEN, INK.*

Gender, Work & Tourism. *M. Thea Sinclair (Ed.)*
Demonstrates how women's work in the world's third largest industry is associated with ideologies of gender and social sexuality.
Routledge, 1997. $22.99

Homeworkers in Global Perspective: Invisible No More. *Eileen Boris and Elisabeth Prügl (Eds.)*
Brings together the voices of policy experts, feminist scholars and homeworkers to provide an in-depth investigation.
Routledge, 1996. $19.99

No Sweat: Fashion, Free Trade and the Rights of Garment Workers. *Andrew Ross (Ed.)*
Workers, activists, labour lawyers, trade unionists and academics challenge the inequities of the new global economy.
Verso, 1997. $17.95

Women, Employment and Exclusion. *Caroline Sweetman (Ed.)*
Examines the main concerns about the employment of women worldwide.
Oxfam, 1996. $12.95

* Contact information on page 146.

You have the right to receive all the benefits and protections while working that men do.

EMPLOYMENT

Your RIGHTS and the

RELEVANT CONVENTIONS

Universal Declaration of Human Rights **(UDHR)**

International Covenant on Economic, Social and Cultural Rights **(ICESCR)**

Convention on the Elimination of All Forms of Discrimination Against Women **(CEDAW)**

International Convention on the Elimination of All Forms of Racial Discrimination **(ICERD)**

Maternity Protection Convention **(MPC)**

Equal Remuneration Convention **(ERC)**

Discrimination (Employment and Occupation) Convention **(DC)**

Workers with Family Responsibilities Convention **(WFRC)**

Convention Concerning Equal Opportunities and Equal Treatment for Men and Women with Family Responsibilities **(CCEO)**

The Home Work Convention **(HWC)** *(not yet entered into force)*

OTHER DOCUMENTS

Declaration on the Elimination of Violence Against Women **(DEVAW)**

UN Fourth World Conference on Women Platform for Action **(PFA)**

Numbers refer to paragraphs in the conventions. To find these conventions see "Where to Find Conventions" in Section 1.

WORKING CONDITIONS

- You have the right to work and to freely choose your job.
  UDHR 23: 1 • ICESCR 6 • ICERD 5e, i • CEDAW 11a ERC 1b • PFA 166 1

- You have the right to work in fair and safe conditions and to be paid enough for an adequate standard of living supplemented by social protections if necessary. Women have the right to the same working conditions as men, especially equal pay for equal work.
  UDHR 23: 2, 3 • ICESCR 7a, b • ICERD 5e: i CEDAW 11, 14: 2e • ERC 2: 1 • PFA 165a, b; 178a, b, c, k • DEVAW 3g

- You have the right to join or form trade unions.
  UDHR 23: 4 • ICCPR 22 • ICESCR 8 • ICERD 5e, ii PFA 165r; 178h, i; 190c

- You have the right to rest and leisure time. You do not have to work unreasonable hours and you have the right to holidays with pay.
  UDHR 24 • ICESCR 7d • CRC 31 • PFA 180a

- Wages will be determined by an objective review of the work.
  ERC 3: 1

- All workers have the right to equal opportunities and treatment.
  DC 2 • PFA 166j

- Children have the right to special protections from economic exploitation, including a minimum age for employment.
  ICESCR 10: 3 • CRC 32 • PFA 166l; 178m, n

PROPERTY AND CREDIT

- You have the right to own goods, land and other property.
  UDHR 17 • CEDAW 16h • ICERD 5d, v

- You have the right to bank loans, mortgages and other forms of financial credit.
  CEDAW 13b • PFA 62; 165e, j; 166a, d

- As a rural woman, you have the right to agricultural credit and loans, marketing facilities, appropriate technology and equal treatment in land and agrarian reform.
  CEDAW 14: 2g • PFA 61b, 62; 166c

MATERNITY RIGHTS

- You have the right to maternity leave with pay or to adequate social security benefits without loss of former employment, seniority or social allowances.
  ICESCR 10: 2 • CEDAW 11: 2b • MPC 4 • PFA 165c

- All employed women regardless of age, nationality, race, creed or marital status are entitled to maternity leave of at least twelve weeks.
  MPC 2, 3

- You cannot be dismissed from your employment because of pregnancy, while on maternity leave or because of your marital status.
  CEDAW 11: 2a • PFA 165c

- You are entitled to special protection at work if you are pregnant.
  CEDAW 11: 2d

- You have the right to receive medical benefits while you are on maternity leave including prenatal confinement and postnatal care.
  MPC 4

36 RIGHTS OF WOMEN

EMPLOYMENT
LAWS that Protect Them

- You shall be given time off during the working day to nurse/breast-feed your baby.

  MPC 5 • PFA 165c

- If you fall ill during your pregnancy and have to take more time off work, you cannot be fired so long as your time off remains within certain limits.

  MPC 3: 5, 6 • PFA 165c

WORKERS WITH FAMILY RESPONSIBILITIES

- Any worker who has dependent family members shall not be discriminated against on the basis of these responsibilities.

  CCEO 3: 1 • PFA 165m

- As far as possible, your state must take measures to enable you to have the freedom to choose employment as well as fair working conditions and social security.

  CCEO 4a, b

- As far as possible, your state must take measures to enable you to have community services such as child care and family services and facilities.

  CEDAW 11: 2c • **CCEO 5a, b** • PFA 173g

- As far as possible, your state must take measures to enable you to have vocational guidance and training that will help you remain integrated in the workforce or reenter the workforce if your family responsibilities cause you to leave it.

  CCEO 7 • PFA 166j

- You cannot be fired because of family responsibilities.

  CCEO 8 • PFA 165c

HOME WORKERS

- Home workers are entitled to equal treatment as wage earners.

  HWC 4 • PFA 165g

- You are protected against discrimination in employment and occupation. You have the right to social security, health benefits, training, and maternity protection. You are also protected by a minimum age for work.

  HWC 4: 2 • PFA 178a, b, c, d

- As a home worker, you have the right to establish or join workers' organizations.

  HWC 4: 2a

- Your work shall be included in national labour statistics.

  HWC 6 • PFA 165g

- National laws and regulations on safety and health at work shall apply to home work, taking into account its special characteristics and establishing conditions under which certain types of work and the use of certain substances may be prohibited.

  HWC 7 • PFA 165g

RELEVANT CONVENTIONS

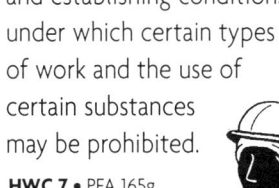

Universal Declaration of Human Rights
(UDHR)

International Covenant on Economic, Social and Cultural Rights
(ICESCR)

Convention on the Elimination of All Forms of Discrimination Against Women
(CEDAW)

International Convention on the Elimination of All Forms of Racial Discrimination
(ICERD)

Maternity Protection Convention
(MPC)

Equal Remuneration Convention
(ERC)

Discrimination (Employment and Occupation) Convention
(DC)

Workers with Family Responsibilities Convention
(WFRC)

Convention Concerning Equal Opportunities and Equal Treatment for Men and Women with Family Responsibilities
(CCEO)

The Home Work Convention
(HWC) *(not yet entered into force)*

OTHER DOCUMENTS

Declaration on the Elimination of Violence Against Women
(DEVAW)

UN Fourth World Conference on Women Platform for Action
(PFA)

Numbers refer to paragraphs in the conventions. To find these conventions see "Where to Find Conventions" in Section 1.

WOMEN AND EMPLOYMENT **37**

Women and

> You have the right to enjoy marriage as an equal partnership.

For millions of women around the world, marriage is anything but a joint and equal partnership.

Many women still do not have the power to decide when and with whom they will marry. Once the wedding ceremony is over, a woman often finds that she has become an appendage of her husband and doesn't have any rights on her own as an individual. She may have to give up her name and nationality, forfeit her right to buy or sell property or enter into contracts, and have to seek her husband's approval in countless everyday transactions. She may not be able to leave the country or take her children out of the country without her husband's permission. Many wives are beaten by their husbands and, without adequate legal protection against domestic violence, they have no tools with which to fight back.

Even in those countries where laws do protect women's rights in marriage, customs often dictate otherwise. Customs, for instance, often encourage child marriages. In India, even though it is against the law, girls are sometimes married at seven or eight years of age. In Bangladesh, 72 percent of girls between 15 and 19 are married, compared with only 7.4 percent of boys. In Nigeria, nearly 25 percent of girls marry before the age of 13.

Early marriage deprives girls of an education and limits their opportunity to have roles outside the home. It prevents women from developing skills that bring them social or economic independence. And it generally results in early and prolonged childbearing, which can undermine the health of both mothers and children.

Polygamy is another marriage practice that is dictated by customs. In Senegal, for example, 64 percent of marriages are polygamous. In some cases—where they are involved in the entire process—women may benefit from polygamy in that it allows them to share their workload. Frequently, how-

38 RIGHTS OF WOMEN

MARRIAGE

ever, a woman's needs and opinions are ignored and the taking of another wife is the business of the husband alone. Consequently, she and her children are forced to live with the economic, social and emotional results.

Women and children suffer further discrimination if they live in countries that do not encourage marriage registration and/or do not recognize de facto relationships. Registration of marriage and the legal recognition of de facto couples can entitle women and children to certain rights. For refugees, registration assures that children born to couples living in countries of asylum are considered legitimate and therefore eligible to a name, nationality, property and economic support. Similarly, the recognition of de facto marriages entitles women to rights of property, inheritance and/or economic support.

While there are two UN conventions that specifically address women's rights within marriage, they have been signed by only a small number of countries. The Convention on the Elimination of All Forms of Discrimination Against Women (CEDAW) and the International Covenant on Civil and Political Rights (ICCPR), however, address many of the issues surrounding marriage, and used in conjunction with the other conventions, can help women activists pressure governments to reform discriminatory laws and practices.

SELECTED PUBLICATIONS
AVAILABLE FROM WOMEN, INK.*

The Burden of Girlhood: A Global Inquiry into the Status of Girls *Neera Kuckreja Sohoni*
Analyses constraints experienced by girls with respect to culture, marriage, health, education, work, violence and affirmative action.
Third Party Publishing, 1995. $19.95

Choose a Future: Issues and Options for Adolescent Girls *CEDPA*
Helps girls and young women examine issues and options in their lives, set goals and develop skills in analysis and decision-making.
Center for Development and Population Activities (CEDPA), 1996. $25.00

Improving the Quality of Life of Girls
Kathleen M. Kurz and Cynthia J. Prather
Examines threats to girls' quality of life, including gender violence, pregnancy and cultural vulnerability faced by teenage girls.
AWID/UNICEF, 1995. $11.95

The State of Women in the World Atlas
Joni Seager
Maps and graphics show the gains that women are making and the many inequalities that persist in a range of areas, including marriage.
Penguin, 1997. $16.95

Where Women Stand: An International Report on the Status of Women in 140 Countries *Naomi Neft and Ann D. Levine*
Highlights the major trends in education, employment, marriage, family planning, health and violence worldwide, plus in-depth profiles of 21 countries.
Random House, 1997. $20.00

* Contact information on page 146.

FACT

So far only 35 countries have signed the international convention that protects a woman's right to choose her own spouse.

FACT

Marriage and childbearing at a young age can permanently injure a girl's health. A study in Bangladesh found the maternal mortality rate of 10- to 14-year-old girls to be five times higher than that of women aged 20 to 24.

MARRIAGE

Your RIGHTS and the

RELEVANT CONVENTIONS

Universal Declaration of Human Rights **(UDHR)**

International Covenant on Civil and Political Rights **(ICCPR)**

International Covenant on Economic, Social and Cultural Rights **(ICESCR)**

Convention on the Elimination of All Forms of Discrimination Against Women **(CEDAW)**

International Convention on the Elimination of All Forms of Racial Discrimination **(ICERD)**

Convention on the Rights of the Child **(CRC)**

Convention on the Nationality of Married Women **(CNMW)**

Convention on Consent to Marriage, Minimum Age for Marriage and Registration of Marriage **(CCM)**

Supplementary Convention on the Abolition of Slavery, the Slave Trade, and Institutions and Practices Similar to Slavery **(SCAS)**

OTHER DOCUMENTS

Declaration on the Elimination of Violence Against Women **(DEVAW)**

UN Fourth World Conference on Women Platform for Action **(PFA)**

Numbers refer to paragraphs in the conventions. To find these conventions see "Where to Find Conventions" in Section 1.

ENTERING MARRIAGE

- You have the same right as a man to freely choose a spouse and enter marriage only with your full consent.
  UDHR 16 • CEDAW 16: 1 • ICCPR 23: 3 • ICESCR 10: 1 CCM 1 • ICERD 5d, iv • SCAS 1c • PFA 274e

- Countries must set a minimum age for marriage. A woman married under that age will not be considered legally married.
  CEDAW 16: 2 • ICCPR 23: 2 • CCM 2 • SCAS 2 PFA 274e

- All marriages must be registered in an official registry.
  CEDAW 16: 2 • CCM 3

- If you marry someone with another nationality, you will not have your nationality automatically changed to that of your husband. Nor will you suddenly find yourself stateless. If you choose, however, you must be granted your husband's nationality.
  CEDAW 9: 1 • CNMW 1, 3

DURING MARRIAGE

- You have the same rights and responsibilities as a man during marriage.
  ICCPR 23: 4 • CEDAW 16: 1

- You have the right to equal access to health care services, including those related to family planning.
  CEDAW 12: 1, 14: 2b; 16: 1e • CRC 24: 2f PFA 106e

- You have the right to protection from violence within the family.
  CEDAW 1 and 16 • DEVAW 2a

- You have the same rights as a man to decide freely about the number and spacing of your children and to have access to the information, education and means to exercise these rights.
  CEDAW 16: 1e • PFA 106i

- You have the same rights and responsibilities as a man towards your children regardless of your marital status.
  CEDAW 16: 1d, f • CRC 18: 1 • PFA 106i

- You have the same rights as a man to family benefits.
  CEDAW 13a

- A change in the nationality of your husband during marriage shall not automatically change your nationality.
  CEDAW 9: 1 • CNMW 1

- You and your husband have equal rights with respect to the nationality of your children.
  CEDAW 9: 2

- You have the same rights as a man to choose a family name, a profession and occupation.
  CEDAW 16: 1g

- If you are employed you must not be discriminated against on the grounds of marriage or maternity.
  CEDAW 11: 2 • PFA 165c

- Countries must ensure that family education includes recognition of maternity as a social function and the recognition of the common responsibility of men and women in the upbringing and development of their children.
  CEDAW 5b• PFA 106g

40 RIGHTS OF WOMEN

MARRIAGE

LAWS that Protect Them

END OF MARRIAGE

- You have the same rights as a man when a marriage ends.
  CEDAW 16: 1c • ICCPR 23: 4

- Neither your nationality, nor that of your children, shall be automatically affected by the ending of a marriage.
  CEDAW 9: 1, 2 • CNMW 1

- You have the same rights and responsibilities as a man towards your children regardless of your marital status.
  CEDAW 16: 1d • CRC 18: 1

"Now that we share the work at home, we have more time to enjoy together."

RELEVANT CONVENTIONS

Universal Declaration of Human Rights
(UDHR)

International Covenant on Civil and Political Rights
(ICCPR)

International Covenant on Economic, Social and Cultural Rights
(ICESCR)

Convention on the Elimination of All Forms of Discrimination Against Women
(CEDAW)

International Convention on the Elimination of All Forms of Racial Discrimination
(ICERD)

Convention on the Rights of the Child
(CRC)

Convention on the Nationality of Married Women
(CNMW)

Convention on Consent to Marriage, Minimum Age for Marriage and Registration of Marriage
(CCM)

Supplementary Convention on the Abolition of Slavery, the Slave Trade, and Institutions and Practices Similar to Slavery
(SCAS)

OTHER DOCUMENTS

Declaration on the Elimination of Violence Against Women
(DEVAW)

UN Fourth World Conference on Women Platform for Action
(PFA)

Numbers refer to paragraphs in the conventions. To find these conventions see "Where to Find Conventions" in Section 1.

WOMEN AND MARRIAGE

Women

You have the right to live as other citizens do, to go to school, to work and to live safely, without fear of abuse.

A refugee, according to the UN Convention Relating to the Status of Refugees, is a person with a well-founded fear of being persecuted based on race, religion, nationality, or membership of a particular social or political group, and who is outside the country of her nationality and is unwilling or unable to return to it because of fear of persecution. This definition, however, does not recognize the countless numbers of people fleeing across international borders for various reasons brought about by increasing ethnic, social and economic instability in their home countries. Nor does it cover the people displaced within their own countries who are in great need of assistance and security.

There are now over 20 million "official" refugees worldwide, nearly ten times more than in 1970, with 80 percent of them women and children. These women and children have been uprooted from their homes and forced to seek refuge and safety in other countries. Another 25 million people are displaced within the borders of their own countries. They are the victims of persecution, ethnic discrimination, human rights abuses, poverty, conflicts and civil strife.

While all refugees and displaced persons are vulnerable, girls and women are particularly so. During their flight, they are often physically abused and raped by border guards, army and resistance units, bandits and male refugees. The physical facilities in refugee camps often provide hopelessly inadequate protection for women. Latrines may be at quite some distance from the living quarters thereby increasing the potential for attacks, especially at night. In camps where men control and allocate rations, women and girls are vulnerable to various forms of sexual blackmail, such as the withholding of food until they have submitted to having sex with the men. Some refugee women and girls are forced into prostitution, providing "sexual services" for soldiers and/or security guards.

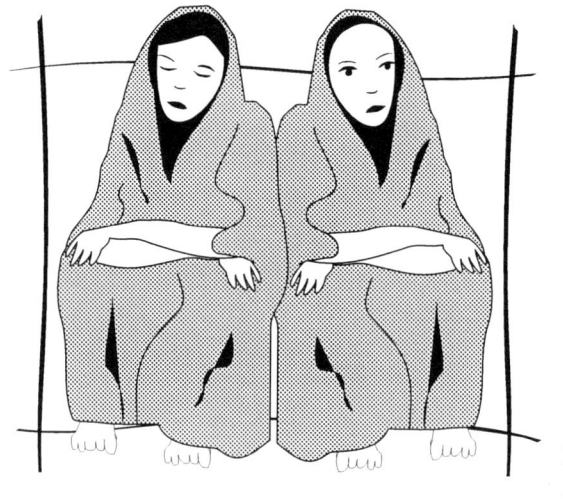

REFUGEES

Meanwhile, refugee women must carry on their multiple responsibilities of caring for the young, the sick and the elderly in unfamiliar and sometimes hostile surroundings. They continue to do their traditional tasks while coping with new environments, new languages, new social and economic roles, new community structures, new familial relationships and possibly overwhelming emotional and physical trauma.

The current UN conventions do not address the specific needs of women refugees. The UN High Commissioner on Refugees has, however, issued several "General Conclusions" that do speak to the rights of women refugees. Although these do not carry the same weight as the conventions, they are included here as important additions to them.

SELECTED PUBLICATIONS
AVAILABLE FROM WOMEN, INK.*

The Human Rights Watch Global Report on Women's Rights
Focuses on the role of governments in perpetuating, condoning and tolerating various kinds of abuse, including sexual abuse of refugee women.
Human Rights Watch Women's Rights Project/ Yale University Press, 1994. $15.00

It's About Time: Human Rights Are Women's Right
HIghlights the situation of women in some 75 countries and addresses women's rights in the context of war as well as the political, economic and social risks they face.
Amnesty International, 1995. $8.95

***Contact information on page 146.**

"
There is no turning back. We've left everything, and all we want is a piece of land without war, a little piece of freedom and perhaps a taste of democracy.
"

— A Bosnian refugee on the Austrian/Slovenian border.

FACT

There are 16 million official refugee women and children—and an estimated 16 million more who are displaced within their own countries.

REFUGEES

Your RIGHTS and the

RELEVANT CONVENTIONS

Universal Declaration of Human Rights **(UDHR)**

Convention Against Torture and Other Cruel, Inhman or Degrading Treatment or Punishment **(CAT)**

International Covenant on Civil and Political Rights **(ICCPR)**

Convention Relating to the Status of Refugees/Protocol Relating to the Status of Refugees **(CRSR)**

Note: The convention was restricted to people who became refugees before 1 January 1951. The protocol extends the provisions of the convention to refugees regardless of when they became refugees.

OTHER DOCUMENTS

United Nations High Commissioner for Refugees **(UNHCR):**
UNHCR General Conclusion 54 **(GC 54)**
UNHCR General Conclusion 60 **(GC 60)**
UNHCR General Conclusion 64 **(GC 64)**
UNHCR General Conclusion 73 **(GC 73)**

UN Fourth World Conference on Women Platform for Action **(PFA)**

Numbers refer to paragraphs in the conventions. To find these conventions see "Where to Find Conventions" in Section 1.

GENERAL PROTECTION

- A refugee is anyone who, owing to a well-founded fear of being persecuted for reasons of race, religion, nationality, or membership of a particular social group or political opinion, is outside the country of her nationality and is unable or unwilling to avail herself of the protection of that country.
  CRSR 1:2

- You have the right to seek asylum from persecution in another country.
  UDHR 14 • ICCPR 13

- You must not be returned to a country if your life or freedom would be threatened because of your race, religion, nationality, social group or political opinion or if you are in danger of being tortured.
  CRSR 33 • CAT 3

- You must not be punished for entering a country illegally, provided you have reported without delay to the authorities and have shown a good reason for your illegal entry.
  CRSR 31

- If you are a refugee, you cannot be expelled without a fair hearing before the law. You must also be given a reasonable period in which to apply for legal admission to another country.
  CRSR 32

RIGHTS IN THE COUNTRY IN WHICH YOU HAVE TAKEN REFUGE

- You have the same rights as national citizens to practice your religion.
  CRSR 4

- You have the right to retain the same personal status, including your marital status, as you enjoyed in your home state.
  CRSR 12

- You have the same rights as other aliens to property, leases and contracts.
  CRSR 13

- You have the same rights as national citizens to join trade unions and nonpolitical and nonprofit associations.
  CRSR 15

- You have the same rights as national citizens to use the justice system.
  CRSR 16
  PFA 147c

- You have the same rights as other aliens to work.
  CRSR 17, 18, 19

- You have the same rights as other aliens to housing.
  CRSR 21

- You have the same rights as other national citizens to elementary education and as aliens to all other levels and types of education as well as to scholarships and the recognition of foreign qualifications.
  CRSR 22

- You have the same rights as nationals to public assistance.
  CRSR 23

- You have the same rights as nationals to receive wages and the benefits of collective bargaining, as well as social security, sickness, injury, maternity, retirement and death benefits.
  CRSR 24

RIGHTS OF WOMEN

REFUGEES

LAWS that Protect Them

- You have the same right to freedom of movement as other aliens.

  CRSR 26

- You must be given the necessary identity papers and travel and administrative documents.

  CRSR 25, 27, 28 • GC 64aviii

- You may transfer the assets you have brought with you to your new country of settlement.

  CRSR 30

ADDITIONAL PROTECTIONS FOR WOMEN REFUGEES

- You have the right to all basic services including food, water, health, sanitation, education and wage-earning opportunities.

  GC 64ix • PFA 147f

- You should be protected from physical dangers, including sexual violence.

  GC 54:2 • GC 60b • GC 73a • PFA 147c

- If you are at risk, you should be given special priority for resettlement.

  GC 54:4; GC 60c; GC 64axi

- If you have suffered sexual abuse you should receive counselling and other services.

  GC 64avi; GC 73f • PFA 147l

- Countries should pass and enforce laws and develop educational materials and training that prevent and combat sexual violence against refugees.

  GC 73b

- Women refugees are an important economic force and need to participate in the planning of refugee protection and assistance programmes.

  GC 54:5 GC 60g; GC 64:2 and ai • PFA 147a

- Women's issues should be included in all plans for refugees.

  GC 54:6; GC 60a and h; ; GC 64av • PFA 147a and o

- To ensure that women and men refugees are treated equally, actions may have to be taken to specifically help women.

  GC 64 para 5 • PFA 226

- Those who have committed crimes against refugee women should be prosecuted.

  GC 64avii

RELEVANT CONVENTIONS

Universal Declaration of Human Rights **(UDHR)**

Convention Against Torture and Other Cruel, Inhman or Degrading Treatment or Punishment **(CAT)**

International Covenant on Civil and Political Rights **(ICCPR)**

Convention Relating to the Status of Refugees/Protocol Relating to the Status of Refugees **(CRSR)**

Note: The convention was restricted to people who became refugees before 1 January 1951. The protocol extends the provisions of the convention to refugees regardless of when they became refugees.

OTHER DOCUMENTS

United Nations High Commissioner for Refugees **(UNHCR):**
UNHCR General Conclusion 54 **(GC 54)**
UNHCR General Conclusion 60 **(GC 60)**
UNHCR General Conclusion 64 **(GC 64)**
UNHCR General Conclusion 73 **(GC 73)**

UN Fourth World Conference on Women Platform for Action **(PFA)**

*Numbers refer to paragraphs in the conventions.
To find these conventions see "Where to Find Conventions" in Section 1.*

SEXUAL EXPLOITATION

You have the right to live and work freely. It is illegal to traffic women for any reason.

Known as the "oldest profession," prostitution is still one of the most profitable for those who manage it. Today the sex trade is a global multibillion-dollar industry. As in other businesses, commodities are traded within and across borders and profits are accumulated and reinvested. In this case the commodities are women, girls and boys—many of whom have been forced into prostitution either by violent coercion or as a result of abject poverty.

The current surge in prostitution and sex trafficking began during the 1960s and 1970s due largely to the global militarism that the Cold War perpetuated. Throughout Southeast Asia and Japan, military build-up brought in hundreds of thousands of troops who quickly became "customers." During the Vietnam War, troops frequenting countries such as Thailand while on rest-and-relaxation leave created a huge and international demand for prostitutes. By the end of the war Ho Chi Minh City alone had 500,000 women prostitutes—a number equal to the total population of the city before the war.

Since the end of the Cold War, sex trafficking has continued as developing nations, in their efforts to attract foreign capital, have built exotic vacation resorts offering an array of natural resources, including tropical foods, picturesque beaches and beautiful women. Sex is often an integral part of the package. Travel brochures for the Philippines and Thailand promise "sun, sea and sex." Tourists arrive by the thousands, and bring much-needed foreign currency into the country. Approximately 75 percent of the five million annual tourists in Thailand are men. Other countries, including Namibia, Zimbabwe, the Ivory Coast, Peru and Brazil, have likewise seen an increase in tourism and, consequently, in the numbers of prostitutes.

No matter what these women and children are called—"cultural entertain-

46 RIGHTS OF WOMEN

AND TRAFFICKING

ers," "hospitality girls," "massage girls"—or where they work, their backgrounds and stories are often similar:. They usually come from poor rural areas and urban slums and, in many cases, they have been either recruited as waitresses or domestic workers or kidnapped and forced into sexual slavery. Sometimes desperate parents sell their daughters to unscrupulous operators out of poverty.

These girls are bought and sold for trifling amounts; some have not reached puberty and do not even know what sex is. They must earn back their selling price to be free, but usually their debt increases to impossible amounts as they are charged for clothes, food and board. Years can go by before they are told that the debt has been paid. By this time the women have no livelihood other than sex work. Recently, with the collapse of their economies, some Eastern European countries have become new sources of women and children who are traded across national borders into countries such as Israel, Lebanon and Turkey.

While the global trafficking of women is most commonly associated with prostitution and sexual bondage, lesser-known forms of trafficking, such as mail-order brides and domestic workers, are equally devastating. The lines between these categories are blurry as mail-order brides and domestic workers become more and more frequently forced into prostitution by their husbands or employers. Mail-order brides and domestic workers are lured by promises of good working conditions overseas, good wages and the prospect of marrying out of existing conditions of poverty. All too often, however, they are forced into a modern form of slavery. Whether they find themselves in exploitative marriages as forced prostitutes or as badly treated domestic workers, their freedoms are curtailed, their labour is exploited and virtually all of their human rights are violated.

How many women are trafficked each year? It's difficult to say with certainty. The United Nations estimates that four million people a year are trafficked. The International Organization for Migration (IOM) reports that 500,000 women a year are trafficked into Western Europe alone. What accounts for these staggering statistics? According to one UN official, trafficking in people has become more profitable than drug trafficking or arms smuggling.

From the boom in bride catalogues

FACT

Trafficking in people has become more profitable than drug trafficking and arms smuggling, according to one UN official.

FACT

In Taiwan, poor farmers, the handicapped and elderly pay intermediaries around $3,000 for a young Vietnamese wife.

— News Report, 1996.

SEXUAL EXPLOITATION AND TRAFFICKING

SEXUAL EXPLOITATION

> *If I beat you it might hurt my hands. If I kill you it will only cost me thirty-five baht to have you buried.*
>
> ---Thai pimp threatening a woman from Burma who had been forced into prostitution in Thailand.

and "introduction" agencies, the business of trafficking does seem to be extremely profitable. The typical buyer/husband is a white man usually looking for a "wife" who will be part servant, part sex partner. These men appear to have no restrictions placed upon them, and can treat their new wives as abusively as they like—especially since these women are legally seen as voluntary participants in their exploitation. Those who are illegal immigrants live under their husbands' constant threats of deportation and have little recourse to justice.

Domestic workers face a similarly bleak situation. They, too, come from poor countries, including Bangladesh, Brazil, Colombia, Ethiopia, Indonesia, Morocco, Nepal, Philippines and Sri Lanka. They are susceptible to low wages, long hours, and physical, sexual and verbal abuse. There are reported cases of domestic workers who are made to kneel before their employers, who have been locked up, who have had their mail intercepted and who have had their wages and passports confiscated. Many domestic servants dream of making enough money to return home but this rarely happens. Instead, they find themselves trapped with little or no legal means of redress.

As with mail-order brides, recruitment agencies make sizeable profits from trafficking domestic workers. Some reports estimate that agencies in Malaysia earn more than US$400,000 per year for the Filipino workers they send abroad and as much as US$850,000 annually for Indonesian workers. One advertisement that ran in the *Singapore Straits Times* illustrates attitudes towards these workers: "Unlimited free replacements, you can't lose, very strict training/control, maids to fit the job specially picked. Why pay more when you can pay less?"

There are many activist women's groups, particularly in Southeast Asia, that are fighting to combat these abus-

AND TRAFFICKING

es, although, sadly, trafficking in women and children is still not as prominent an issue as it should be. Moreover, this area is inadequately covered by human rights conventions. Those conventions that specifically address it urgently need to be rewritten. For example, activists believe that the Convention for the Suppression of the Traffic in Persons and of the Exploitation of the Prostitution of Others (CSTPEP) has, on the one hand, gone too far because it completely outlaws prostitution whether it be forced or consensual. At the same time, this convention contains several paragraphs that restrict women's freedom.

The best protections are found in the UN Fourth World Conference on Women Platform for Action and the Declaration on the Elimination of Violence Against Women which, as described earlier in this section, are not legally binding. However, they do establish a moral standard and can be used as organizing and mobilizing tools. On the next page we have included all of the above so that women can turn these international commitments into a springboard for action.

SELECTED PUBLICATIONS
AVAILABLE FROM WOMEN, INK.*

Stolen Lives: Trading Women into Sex and Slavery *Sietske Altink*
Gives a history of trafficking and documents why and how women are hired, transported and trapped into prostitution.
Haworth Press, 1996. $17.95

The Traffic in Women: Human Realities of the International Sex Trade *Siriporn Skrobanek, Nattaya Boonpakdee and Chutima Jantateroo*
Brings to light the nature and extent of the problem worldwide and shows how women can be empowered to end the traffic.
Zed Books, 1997. $17.50

Trafficking in Women: Forced Labour and Slavery-like Practices in Marriage, Domestic Labour and Prostitution *Marjan Wijers and Lin Lap-Chew*
Discusses the international laws that do, and do not, protect women against abuses and offers concrete recommendations to combat trafficking.
Foundation Against Trafficking in Women/Global Alliance Against Traffic in Women, 1997. $20.00

Women's Rights, Human Rights: International Feminist Perspectives *Andrea Wolper and Julie S. Peters*
Shows how the women's human rights movement has transformed the prevailing notion of rights, with a focus on trafficking, among other topics.
Routledge, 1994. $24.99

* **Contact information on page 146.**

FACT

There are more than 700 marriage brokers importing Asian women to Japan. Matchmaking fees run as high as US$20,000.

— Debbie Taylor, "Servile Marriage: A Definition, a Survey, and the Start of a Campaign for Change."
Oxford, UK, 1993.

SEXUAL EXPLOITATION

Your RIGHTS and the

RELEVANT CONVENTIONS

Universal Declaration of Human Rights
(UDHR)

International Covenant on Civil and Political Rights
(ICCPR)

International Covenant on Economic, Social and Cultural Rights
(ICESCR)

Convention on the Rights of the Child
(CRC)

Convention on the Elimination of All Forms of Discrimination Against Women
(CEDAW)

Supplementary Convention on the Abolition of Slavery, the Slave Trade and Institutions and Practices Similar to Slavery
(SCAS)

Convention for the Suppression of the Traffic in Persons and of the Exploitation of the Prostitution of Others
(CSTPEP)

OTHER DOCUMENTS

Declaration on the Elimination of Violence Against Women
(DEVAW)

UN Fourth World Conference on Women Platform for Action
(PFA)

Numbers refer to paragraphs in the conventions. To find these conventions see "Where to Find Conventions" in Section 1.

PREVENTING SEXUAL EXPLOITATION AND TRAFFICKING

- You have the right to protection from all forms of traffic in women and children for the purposes of prostitution or any other forms of exploitation.
  CEDAW 6 • CRC 35, 36 • SCAS 1Ci • PFA 230n

- Countries should condemn and put an end to violence against women, including trafficking and forced prostitution.
  DEVAW 2b

- No one has the right to enslave anyone else. Slavery is a crime.
  UDHR 4 • ICCPR 8 • SCAS 3: 1

- Countries should take all measures to stop debt bondage, serfdom, the marriage trade and the selling of children.
  SCAS 1

- Countries shall take all measures to prevent ships bearing their flags from carrying slaves.
  SCAS 3: 2

- Countries must take measures to prevent prostitution through educational, health, economic and other services.
  CSTPEP 16

- Countries must publicize the dangers of trafficking.
  CSTPEP 17: 2

- Countries must watch railway stations, airports, seaports and transportation to prevent the international trafficking of people.
  CSTPEP 17: 3 • SCAS 3: 2b

PUNISHING SEXUAL EXPLOITATION AND TRAFFICKING

- Countries shall impose severe penalties for anyone bringing slaves from one country to another.
  SCAS 3: 1

- Countries shall punish anyone shipping slaves under that country's flag.
  SCAS 3: 2

- Countries must punish anyone who either forces or persuades another person into prostitution, even if that person agrees.
  CSTPEP 1 • PFA 130

- Countries must punish anyone who profits from the prostitution of another person, even if that person consents.
  CSTPEP 1 • PFA 130

- Countries must punish anyone who owns, manages or finances a brothel.
  CSTPEP1

- Countries must punish anyone who knowingly rents space to people involved in prostitution.
  CSTPEP 2

- Countries must work with other countries to produce information that will lead to the punishment of traffickers.
  CSTPEP 15 • SCAS 3, 8 • PFA 130

- Countries should increase cooperation between law enforcement authorities to break trafficking rings.
  PFA 130

AND TRAFFICKING

LAWS that Protect Them

- Countries should punish those who subject women to violence.

  DEVAW 4d

HELP FOR VICTIMS OF SEXUAL EXPLOITATION AND TRAFFICKING

- As a victim of forced prostitution, you have the right to rehabilitation.

  CSTPEP 16 • DEVAW 4g

- If you have been trafficked, you have the right to programmes that offer job training, health care and psychological services.

  PFA 130

SEXUAL EXPLOITATION AND TRAFFICKING OF CHILDREN

- Countries must take measures to fight trafficking of children.

  CRC 35

- Countries must take all measures to protect children from exploitation and sexual abuse.

  CRC 19, 34

- Children have a right to protection from economic exploitation and from doing any work that is harmful to their physical, mental, moral or spiritual development.

  CRC 32: 1

- Children have the right to be protected from sexual exploitation and abuse, including unlawful sexual activity, prostitution and pornography.

  CRC 34 • PFA 230m, 283b

CHILDREN HAVE THE RIGHT TO BE PROTECTED FROM SEXUAL EXPLOITATION

RELEVANT CONVENTIONS

Universal Declaration of Human Rights
(UDHR)

International Covenant on Civil and Political Rights
(ICCPR)

International Covenant on Economic, Social and Cultural Rights
(ICESCR)

Convention on the Rights of the Child
(CRC)

Convention on the Elimination of All Forms of Discrimination Against Women
(CEDAW)

Supplementary Convention on the Abolition of Slavery, the Slave Trade and Institutions and Practices Similar to Slavery
(SCAS)

Convention for the Suppression of the Traffic in Persons and of the Exploitation of the Prostitution of Others
(CSTPEP)

OTHER DOCUMENTS

Declaration on the Elimination of Violence Against Women
(DEVAW)

UN Fourth World Conference on Women Platform for Action
(PFA)

*Numbers refer to paragraphs in the conventions.
To find these conventions see "Where to Find Conventions" in Section 1.*

Women and

You have the right to be free from torture or any other cruel or dehumanizing treatment.

Torture. To many people this word brings to mind images of beatings, electric shocks or brutal interrogations. But hundreds of thousands of women experience another kind of torture as well: sexual torture inflicted and permitted, indeed considered standard procedure, by policemen, military personnel and prison guards. Sexual torture may include forced vaginal, anal and oral penetration, inappropriate touching and fondling, strip-searches and the use of sexualized language.

Human Rights Watch has documented cases of and published reports on sexual torture in countries as seemingly disparate as the United States, Egypt and Pakistan. In the United States, male correction officers have been reported to grope female prisoners while frisking them and to watch (or even videotape) them being strip-searched. In Egypt, security forces have been known to detain relatives of suspected Islamic militants and threaten to rape them unless their family members give themselves up. They have also stripped women naked and placed them in rooms with naked male detainees in order to further degrade them. According to local human rights lawyers in Pakistan, more than 70 percent of women in police custody experience physical torture, including sexual abuse. They report that police personnel have been found to participate in gang rapes and to insert objects—such as police batons and chili peppers—into female prisoners' vaginas and rectums.

Women are especially vulnerable to torture during times of war and internal conflict, when their bodies are seen as the legitimate instruments and spoils of war. Amnesty International states that ". . . women are being raped—terrorized, degraded and violated—in every modern conflict on the planet." Particularly outrageous are the mass rapes and forced impregnations that have been reported most recently in Bangladesh, Haiti, Kashmir, India, Kenya, Peru,

TORTURE

Rwanda, Somalia and the former Yugoslavia.

In 1996, the International Criminal Tribunal for the former Yugoslavia charged several Bosnian Serb military, paramilitary and police officers with using rape as an instrument of torture. This was the first time in history that rape had been charged as a war crime. The decision to bring this charge was a landmark victory for women everywhere.

In addition to demanding that rape and other sexual abuses by those in power be considered torture, activists have been arguing that domestic violence can also be a form of torture that should be recognized. This involves a broadening of the understanding of torture so that it includes actions by people who are not officials of the state. By not protecting women from domestic violence, activists point out, the state is responsible and accountable for daily acts of torture in the home. With the legal backing of the conventions on the following page, they hope to bring new attention to gender-specific torture and enable women to claim one of the most fundamental human rights of all—the right to live without fear.

SELECTED PUBLICATIONS
AVAILABLE FROM WOMEN, INK.*

The Human Rights Watch Global Report on Women's Rights
Focuses on the role of governments in perpetuating, condoning and tolerating various kinds of abuse, including rape as a tactic of war and political repression.
Human Rights Watch, 1995. $15.00

It's About Time: Human Rights Are Women's Right
Highlights the situation of women in some 75 countries and addresses women's rights in various contexts, including war.
Amnesty International, 1995. $8.95

* Contact information on page 146.

FACT

The people most frequently abused by officials are among the world's most marginalized groups: indigenous, refugee or displaced women. In Mexico, for example, three Tzeltal sisters, ages 16, 18 and 20, were brutally raped by soldiers in 1994 following an indigenous peasant uprising.

TORTURE

.... Your RIGHTS and the LAWS that Protect Them

RELEVANT CONVENTIONS

Universal Declaration of Human Rights
(UDHR)

International Covenant on Civil and Political Rights
(ICCPR)

Convention on the Rights of the Child
(CRC)

Convention Against Torture and Other Cruel, Inhuman or Degrading Treatment or Punishment
(CAT)

OTHER DOCUMENTS

Declaration on the Elimination of Violence Against Women
(DEVAW)

Declaration on the Protection of Women and Children in Emergency and Armed Conflict
(DPWCEAC)

UN Fourth World Conference on Women Platform for Action
(PFA)

Numbers refer to paragraphs in the conventions. To find these conventions see "Where to Find Conventions" in Section 1.

DEFINING AND PREVENTING TORTURE

- Torture is the intentional infliction of severe pain or suffering, either physical or mental, by anyone acting in an official capacity for the purpose of getting information, forcing a confession, punishment, intimidation, coercion or discrimination of any kind.
  CAT 1

- You shall not be subjected to torture or to cruel, inhuman or degrading treatment or punishment.
  UDHR 5 • ICCPR 7 • CRC 37a • CAT 12
  DEVAW 2c; 3h

- You cannot be subjected to medical or scientific experimentation against your will.
  ICCPR 7

- A country cannot use war, internal conflict or any public emergency as an excuse for torture. A person cannot use orders from a superior as a reason for torture.
  CAT 2

- You cannot be forced to return to a country where you may be in danger of torture.
  CAT 3

- You and your children have a right to protection in situations of armed conflict against rape, forced prostitution, persecution, torture, punitive measures, degrading treatment, violence and any other form of assault and sexual slavery.
  PFA 144b • DPWCEAC 4

PUNISHING TORTURE

- All acts of torture are criminal offences and shall face appropriate penalties.
  CAT 4, 5 • DEVAW 4c, d • PFA 145c, d, e

- Police officers, prison officials, medical personnel, military and other public officials shall not use torture in law enforcement.
  CAT 10, 11

HELP FOR TORTURE VICTIMS

- You have the right to seek justice for violence you have suffered. If you are being or have been tortured, you have the right to complain; your complaints shall be promptly and impartially investigated and you shall be protected.
  CAT 12, 13 • DEVAW 4d

- As a victim of violence or torture, you are entitled to full redress. You or your dependents have the right to compensation and rehabilitation. If the torture victim has died, her or his dependents are entitled to compensation.
  CAT 14

- Child victims of armed conflict, torture or maltreatment have the right to measures that promote physical and psychological recovery and social reintegration.
  CRC 39

3

Developing Rights

IN THIS SECTION

Redefining Women's Human Rights
- Violence Against Women
- Housing, Land and Property
- Reproductive Rights
- Environmental Rights
- Women with Disabilities
- Sexual Orientation Rights

Redefining Women's Human Rights

Understanding international laws is just a first step. In order to become true champions of our human rights we must also become involved in making these laws. You may be thinking, "How can I do that if I am not a lawyer?" Or, "What kind of laws could I write when there are so many laws already?"

As any woman who has suffered an injustice knows, the laws that exist are not adequate. They are not adequate because they reflect the particular political, social, and economic perspective of those who wrote them. Who writes the majority of international and national laws? Men who are not conscious of the needs of women; well-off lawmakers who have never experienced poverty. As a result, the laws that cover a particular human rights issue—access to land and credit for example—do not sufficiently address the obstacles that women living in poverty experience. So while there are countless documents codifying the human rights of individuals, there remain numerous issues that have yet to be adequately addressed by human rights law.

Not only are there issues that receive insufficient attention, but there are many issues that have yet to be defined as human rights violations by lawmakers. This is primarily because these issues have not been defined as human rights violations by the people who are affected by them. Domestic violence is a case in point. For a long time, women themselves regarded this as a private matter—something outside the scope of the law. Even when women finally began to recognize violence in the home as a crime, they did not at first consider it specifically a human rights crime. In fact, the Convention on the Elimination of All Forms of Discrimination Against Women (CEDAW), considered the most important human rights document for women, fails to explicitly focus on the problem; at the time CEDAW was written, women activists and lawmakers did not consider domestic violence to be a human rights concern.

Today, activists and lawmakers worldwide recognize violence in the home as a human rights issue. What does it take to gain such recognition? First, an injustice must be understood as a human rights issue by the people who have suffered it. But that alone is not enough. Those who have suffered must then be able to make their suffering known. Unfortunately, too often those who have experienced a human rights violation do not have the economic resources or political access to make the violation visible.

Even when a human rights issue is made

visible, there are still many obstacles to seeing it addressed in legal documents. First, there is often philosophical, economic, and/or legal disagreement about the role of the state in providing basic necessities such as shelter and education. In poorer countries particularly, there is the question of how limited resources are allocated. Financial realities determine whose human rights are defended, and resources tend to go to those with the strongest political and economic power. In no country is women's power sufficiently strong.

Second there is philosophical, economic, and legal disagreement about government's role in regulating the private lives of its citizens. Customs dictate many practices that violate women's human rights and many government leaders do not have the political will or financial resources to combat these violations.

Given all these factors, what are the next steps to ensure that the violations against women are recognized as human rights violations and addressed by international laws? In these final years of the 20th century, most legal experts agree that it is unlikely the United Nations will be adopting new conventions in the near future. So without the benefit of international conventions, women have begun to employ a wide variety of other strategies to champion these rights. (To learn about the convention process itself, see Section 1: "Understanding Conventions.") These strategies include:

MAKING WOMEN'S RIGHTS VIOLATIONS VISIBLE ON A LOCAL LEVEL

- At local, regional and country levels, women are building pressure from the bottom up by bringing violations to public attention and thus forcing governments to recognize and protect women's human rights. A tribunal campaign, which uses mass media to publicize women's human rights violations, is one approach that has proven to be particularly successful. (For further information, see 'A Tribunal' in Section 4)

- In places where it is difficult for women to organize publicly, to access the media, or to counter a well-orchestrated opposition, contacts with regional and international human rights networks are key to increasing visibility of women's rights violations. This is particularly true in countries where fundamentalist forces are powerful. The Women Living Under Muslim Laws network, for example, which works with groups in 28 predominantly Muslim countries, has used action alerts to mobilize a chorus of protest from both within and without the Muslim world. These alerts help bring attention to human rights violations that would otherwise remain invisible or tacitly sanctioned by the various governments.

DEVELOPING RIGHTS 57

BRINGING WOMEN'S RIGHTS VIOLATIONS TO INTERNATIONAL FORA

- Activists have been insisting that women's human rights figure prominently on the agenda at regional, national and international conferences. The UN World Conference on, held in Istanbul in June 1996, is a good example. At that conference the particular obstacles women face in securing adequate housing were a central discussion point and were included in the policy documents and recommendations that evolved from the conference.

- Women have also been lobbying the UN General Assembly to recognize and allocate sufficient funds and programmes for women's issues. For instance, it was due to the pressure of a coalition of women's organizations that 1975 was designated as International Women's Year. This subsequently led to the designation of an entire 10-year period, the UN Decade for Women 1976-1985, when governments were called upon to make special efforts to address the obstacles confronting women in their daily lives.

ENSURING THAT WOMEN HELP TO FORMULATE INTERNATIONAL POLICY

- Women from all over the world participated in the writing of the Beijing Platform for Action, thanks to a region-wide, broad-based preparatory process that encouraged women to engage in policy-making. Similarly, during the years leading up to the 1994 UN International Conference on Population and Development in Cairo, a global women's health coalition was responsible for asserting the primacy of women's reproductive rights in the formulation of the policy document that was to emerge from this conference.

- Women are lobbying to change the gender composition of law and decision-making bodies and to appoint individuals responsible for addressing gender issues (with adequate financial resources to back their actions). The Special Rapporteur on Violence Against Women was appointed because of global pressure at the 1993 World Conference on Human Rights in Vienna.

- Activists are also insisting that experts on gender be given a chance to cooperate with and monitor the work of the UN committees of particular relevance to women. This is the case with the Women's Caucus for Gender Justice, which has been working with the UN committee charged with the creation of the International Criminal Court in an effort to ensure that a gender perspective is reflected in every aspect of the proceedings.

- Women are campaigning for better procedures that would enable women to bring complaints of human rights violations to the appropriate authorities. This is best exemplified by the women lawyers and activists who are urging the passage of an Optional Protocol to the Convention on the Elimination of All Forms of Discrimination Against Women (CEDAW).

PRESSING FOR NEW INTERPRETATIONS OF EXISTING LAWS

- Women are encouraging new interpretations of existing international conventions (e.g. for rape during wartime to be understood as a form of torture) and lobbying for supplementary UN documents that address women's issues (the passage of the Declaration Against Violence Against Women is a good example).

- Women who are experts in their fields are also contributing to the formation of new UN documents that offer gender perspectives. With pressure and input from housing activists, for instance, the UN Sub-Commission on the Prevention of Discrimination and on the Protection of Minorities has adopted a resolution that describes women's right to land and adequate housing.

This section shows how women have employed these strategies in the following human rights issues: housing, land and property; violence against women; reproductive rights; environmental rights; disability rights; and sexual orientation. To find any UN documents mentioned in this section, see "Where to Find Conventions" (page 15).

"Why are women re-interpreting existing human rights laws? Aren't women and men both equally human?"

"Well sure we're equally human! But existing laws frequently do not have a gender perspective and have disregarded important issues such as rape in times of war."

DEVELOPING RIGHTS **59**

Housing, Land

CONTACTS

AFRICA
Action Aid
431 av. 24 de Julho
Maputo, **MOZAMBIQUE**
Tel: (258-1) 49-36-41
Contact: Rachel Waterhouse

Centre on Governance and Development
P.O. Box 60043
Nairobi, **KENYA**
Tel: (254) 4-32-19
Fax: (254) 4-12-50
E-mail: <mswahili@nbet.co.ke>
Contact: Murtaza Jaffer

Habitat International
Coalition/Women and Shelter
P.O. Box 5914
Dar es Salaam, **TANZANIA**
Tel: (255-51) 18-47-57
Fax: (255-51) 11-25-38
E-mail: <wat@ud.co.tz>
Contact: Tabitha Siwale

Mazingira Institute
P.O. Box 14550
Nairobi, **KENYA**
Tel: (254-2) 44-32-26/9
Fax: (254-2) 44-46-43
E-mail:
<mazingira@elci.sasa.unep.org>
Contact: Diana Lee-Smith

UN Centre for Human Settlements,
Women and Habitat
P.O. Box 30030
Nairobi, **KENYA**
Tel: (254-2) 62-30-31
E-mail:
<catalina.trujillo@unchs.org>
Contact: Catalina Trujillo

National Land Committee
P.O. Box 30944
Braamfontein 2017
SOUTH AFRICA
Tel: (27-11) 403-3803
Fax: (27-11) 339-6315
E-mail: <ncc@wn.apc.org>
Contact: Melanie Samson

The right to housing is a fundamental human right, codified in the earliest human rights documents. Women's specific right to housing and the related right of women to own, administer and manage property has been described in the Convention on the Elimination of All Forms of Discrimination Against Women. More recently, the Committee on Economic, Social and Cultural Rights (set up by ECOSOC to have the responsibility of interpreting and monitoring the International Covenant on Economic, Social and Cultural Rights) has further defined the right to housing as the right to a place for everyone to live in peace and dignity. The housing must be affordable, liveable, secure and located in a safe area. To enjoy the right to housing, one must have access to materials and infrastructure and the legal security to occupy that house.

Despite these international documents, local custom, recession-stricken economies, war and internal conflicts, and violence against women have all conspired to leave millions of women with extremely inadequate, insanitary and insecure housing and living conditions that directly threaten their mental and physical health and overall well-being. Women activists, alarmed by the large numbers of homeless, propertyless and landless women, have been working effectively to place all of these issues on the international human rights agenda.

At both the 1996 World Conference on Habitat in Istanbul in 1996 and the 1995 UN Fourth World Conference on Women in Beijing, for instance, activists promoted discussion of the issues that are relevant to women's right to housing. While neither of the documents coming out of these conferences specifically refers to housing as a women's right, both identify the central barriers that women face in relation to housing: poverty and the feminization of poverty, discrimination in accessing and maintaining housing, barriers to renting and owning land and property, gender-biased access to economic resources,

and Property

domestic violence and barriers to participation in the housing process.

Thanks to the attention brought to these issues at the 1995 and 1996 world conferences, in 1997 one of the sub-commissions of the Commission on Human Rights adopted the first UN resolution on women and the right to adequate housing and to land and property. The ECOSOC committee is expected to follow in the near future with a general comment on what the right to housing means for women.

In the meantime, activists are working on several fronts, using these international documents as lobbying tools to press national governments to repeal or amend discriminatory property and inheritance laws and policies; to adopt new laws and policies that ensure women's right to own, rent and inherit property and land without discrimination; and to address the issue of violence against women during forced eviction, particularly when eviction is used as a strategy of war. Finally they are campaigning for women's participation in every aspect of the housing process, from the planning, design and construction of housing, to the development and implementation of grassroots local and national housing rights movements.

RELEVANT CONVENTIONS AND DOCUMENTS

Universal Declaration of Human Rights 25:1

International Covenant on Economic, Social and Cultural Rights
Article 11: 1.

Convention on the Elimination of All Forms of Discrimination Against Women 14:2 h, 16:1h

UN Fourth World Conference on Women Platform for Action

Habitat Conference policy document

The Sub-Commission on the Prevention of Discrimination and Protection of Minorities Resolution on Women and the Right to Adequate Housing and to Land and Property

This resolution defines the type of gender discrimination that threatens women's right to adequate housing, land and property, recognizes the issue of violence against women as it relates to housing, land and property rights and makes specific recommendations for ways to uphold women's rights in these areas.

CONTACTS

ASIA/PACIFIC
Centre on Housing Rights & Eviction, Women's Programme
5/43 Broadway, Elwood,
Vic. 3184, **AUSTRALIA**
Tel/Fax: (61-3) 9531-2773
E-mail: <farwise@ibm.net>
Contact: Leilani Farha

University of the Philippines
Center for Women's Studies
E. Jacinta St. Dilimai
Quezon City, **PHILIPPINES**
Tel: (63-2) 929-1637
Contact: Asteya Santiago

LATIN AMERICA
Organizacion de Mujeres Guatemales
2 Avenida 2-78 Zona Uno
Guatemala City, **GUATEMALA**
Contact: Maria Hernandez

MIDDLE EAST
Palestine Human Rights Info. Centre
P.O. Box 51090
Jerusalem, **via ISRAEL**
Tel: (972-2) 628-7076
Contact: Jihad Abu Zneid

NORTH AMERICA
Centre for Equality Rights
in Accomodation
517 College St. Suite 408
Toronto, ONT M6G 4A2
CANADA
Tel: (1-416) 944-0087
Fax: (1-416) 944-1803
E-mail: <cera@web.net>
Contact: Bruce Porter

Land Tenure Center
University of Wisconsin
1357 University Avenue
Madison, WI 53715, **USA**
Te: (1-608) 262-0097
Fax: (1-608) 262-2141
E-mail: <Susana@macc.wisc.edu>

Violence Against

FACT

Between 20 and 27 percent of college-aged women in five high-income countries report being victims of rape or attempted rape.

Violence against women is not explicitly mentioned in the Convention on the Elimination of All Forms of Discrimination Against Women (CEDAW). Since the convention's entry into force in 1981, however, violence against women in both the private and public spheres has emerged as one of the most pressing issues to be addressed by the international community.

Indeed, because of pressure from regional, national and international activists, violence against women has been explicitly and strongly condemned during several UN-sponsored global conferences, including the 1985 World Conference on Women in Nairobi, the 1993 World Conference on Human Rights in Vienna and the 1995 Fourth World Conference on Women in Beijing.

Moreover, activists succeeded in pressuring the UN to adopt a Declaration on the Elimination of All Forms of Violence Against Women in late 1993 and to appoint a Special Rapporteur on Violence Against Women, an official whose mandate is to uncover and address the vast dimensions of the problem. Although the Declaration is not legally binding, it is a statement that has considerable moral weight and may

RELEVANT DOCUMENTS

- **Declaration on the Elimination of Violence Against Women**

- **CEDAW General Recommendation 12,** adopted by the Committee that monitors the Convention on the Elimination of All Forms of Discrimination Against Women (CEDAW).

  This recommendation states that the Committee considers gender-based violence to be a form of gender discrimination, and therefore outlawed by CEDAW.

- **CEDAW General Recommendation 14,** adopted by the Committee that monitors the Convention on the Elimination of All Forms of Discrimination Against Women (CEDAW).

  This recommendation calls on governments to eradicate female genital mutilation.

- **UN Fourth World Conference on Women Platform for Action**
  One of the 12 areas of critical concern, violence against women is well-addressed in the PFA. See paragraphs 112-130. Women and armed conflict is another area of concern. See paragraphs 131-149.

- **The Fourth Geneva Convention**
  Relative to the Treatment of Civilian Persons in Time of War. Article 47 of this documents prohibits wartime rape and enforced prostitution.

Women

become law in the future. The Declaration recognizes instances of violence against women in three spheres:

- in families, which includes battering, sexual abuse of female children, dowry-related violence, marital rape, female genital mutilation, nonspousal violence and violence related to exploitation;

- in communities, which includes rape, sexual abuse, sexual harassment at work and in educational institutions, trafficking in women and forced prostitution. (For more on this see "Sexual Exploitation and Trafficking" in Section 2); and

- violence that is perpetrated or condoned by the state, including armed conflict.

Within these spheres, the instances of violence that have been receiving a great amount of attention internationally are domestic violence, female genital mutilation, violence due to preference for males and sexual violence during armed conflict.

DOMESTIC VIOLENCE

Violence in the home is predominantly male violence directed against women and children, and is of pandemic proportions. However, despite its prevalence, domestic violence was not recognized as a human rights violation partly because it occurs in the privacy of the home and family relations. Further, it is a problem that has been largely invisible because many women victims are reluctant to speak out because of shame, or fear of further violence, or because they believe it is a normal and acceptable part of married life. Therefore, change needs to take place at many levels.

In arguing that human rights law should play a role in the eradication of domestic violence, a key question is how to hold states responsible for human rights abuses perpetrated not by the state itself but by private actors. Activists and international lawmakers are using different approaches to address this question. One approach is to argue that states' responsibility for human rights violations should not be confined to violations that result from the actions of the state and its officials or agents, but also include those that result from states' inaction. According to this line of thinking, where states have not taken measures to combat domestic violence, they should be held internationally accountable.

Another approach, taken by the CEDAW Committee in its General Recommendation 12, is that gender-based violence in the home infringes on women's right to equality in the family and is therefore illegal gender discrimination.

A third approach, adopted by the

> **FACT**
>
> *130 million women worldwide are estimated to have undergone female genital mutilation, with an additional two million girls and women undergoing the procedure every year.*

Declaration on the Elimination of Violence Against Women, is that violence occurring in the family is an aspect of the systematic subordination of women by men and therefore is, in and of itself, a human rights violation in the same way as torture is.

FEMALE GENITAL MUTILATION

The practice of female genital mutilation is deeply engrained in some local and national traditions of femininity. This makes it a very complex issue for human rights activists as many of the "victims" do not see themselves as such. Activists are engaged in important debates about whether the legal system is an appropriate way to address this problem, and whether there is any role for feminist activists from the Global North to play. The alternative is to work with, and/or provide resources for, local women's organizations and government agencies to educate communities about the substantial health risks and the devastating effects on women's sexuality that arise from female genital mutilation. Perhaps the answer is that both legal and nonlegal strategies are necessary, and that both must be carefully employed so as to ensure that the women who are directly affected participate in the process and are not in any way disempowered by it.

There is not even agreement about the terminology that should be employed to describe the practice. The CEDAW Committee refers to it as "female circumcision" in General Comment 11 and suggests that states take preventive actions related to women's education and health rights. Meanwhile the DEVAW uses the term "female genital mutilation" and suggests a range of strategies to eradicate violence against women, including punishing those public and private actors responsible.

In December 1997, Egypt's highest court made a significant decision when it upheld legislation introduced in 1996 that banned the "genital cutting" of women and girls. Importantly, the court said that there was nothing in Islamic law that condoned the practice. The court's decision provides a powerful weapon for Egyptian women's groups who do not support the practice, and may have positive reverberations in other Islamic nations and communities.

PREFERENCE FOR MALES

When parents have a strong preference for their children to be sons, the results can be disastrous for girls, including higher rates of mortality, nutritional deprivation, little access to education or health care. Preference for males, along with prenatal sex selection, have also been tied to female infanticide, forced sterilization and abortion, female genital mutilation, child marriages and forced prostitution.

SEXUAL VIOLENCE DURING ARMED CONFLICT

Increasingly, most of the victims of war are not soldiers, but civilians. Their treatment is often extremely harsh. Both female and male civilians are liable to be shot, hung, burned, stabbed, beaten, bombed, tortured and forced into slave labour. However, women suffer additional atrocities that happen far less often to men. Whereas male civilians may be killed, women are often raped first and then killed. Whereas male civilians may be tortured, women are often both raped and then tortured in other ways also. Furthermore, during wartime women are often forced to act as prostitutes, forcibly sterilized so they cannot have children, forcibly impregnated, forced to bear children, sexually mutilated and sexually assaulted. Women and girls may be kidnapped in order to serve as sexual and domestic slaves. (During World War II, for example, tens of thousands of women from all over Asia were forced into sexual slavery and served as "comfort women" to Japanese soldiers.) And contrary to popular views, the perpetrators are not only members of the military, but members of the government, civilians, medical personnel and journalists. Even if women find a way to flee, they often find discrimination and sexual violence equally brutal in the refugee camps.

The laws of war, called humanitarian laws, are meant to provide protections for civilians in war. They forbid sexual assault, as do domestic military and civil codes. Additionally, since 1949, article 47 of the Fourth Geneva Convention Relative to the Treatment of Civilian Persons in Times of War explicitly prohibits wartime rape and enforced prostitution; these prohibitions were reinforced in 1977 by Additional Protocols to the 1949 Geneva Conventions. Despite these laws, in the past sexual assault crimes were generally ignored and treated as an inevitable by-product of war.

However, positive signs are emerging that crimes against women in war will no longer be ignored. The UN set up two short-term war crimes tribunals, one for crimes committed in the former Yugoslavia (1993) and one for crimes committed during the Rwandan genocide (1994). These two tribunals have charged war criminals with such gender-based crimes as rape and sexual slavery. The two tribunals have also recognized that rape may be one of the crimes used in genocide and should be considered a form of torture. A treaty setting up a permanent International Criminal Court was also adopted by a vote of 120 countries in Rome in July 1998 to rule on genocide, crimes against humanity and war crimes, but has yet to come into force as of this writing.

Resources/Contacts

BOOKS

SELECTED PUBLICATIONS
AVAILABLE FROM WOMEN, INK.*

Female Genital Mutilation: A Call to Global Action *Nahid Toubia*
A compelling overview of the global prevalence of female genital mutilation.
Rainbo, 1995 (second edition). $9.95

Gender Violence and Women's Human Rights in Africa
Presents ideas and strategies from some of Africa's foremost human rights activists.
Center for Women's Global Leadership, 1994. $7.00

States Responses to Domestic Violence: Current Status and Needed Improvements
An overview of current legal responses to domestic violence with a model for drafting legislation.
Women, Law and Development International, 1996. $10.00

STOP Female Genital Mutilation: Women Speak: Facts and Actions *Fran P. Hosken*
Provides an overview of developments to halt FGM, looking particularly at grassroots initiatives.
WIN News, 1995. $15.00

Strategies for Confronting Domestic Violence: A Resource Manual
Examines the nature, causes and prevention of domestic violence and details ways in which the problem can be confronted.
UN Publications, 1993. $19.95

Violence Against Women: New Movements and New Theories in India *Gail Omvedt*
Describes and explains the nature of violence against women in India.
Kali for Women, 1990. $6.95

Women Against Violence: Breaking the Silence *Ana Maria Brasileiro (Ed.)*
Documents the different types of violence experienced in various cultures and contexts and the steps women are taking to end it.
UNIFEM, 1997. $9.95

Women and Violence: Realities and Responses Worldwide *Miranda Davies (Ed.)*
Case studies from over 30 countries examine the incidence of different types of violence, from child sexual abuse to rape in wartime.
Zed Press, 1994. 17.50

* Contact information on page 146.

CONTACTS

ONLINE CONTACTS

Human Rights Watch
This organization monitors human rights violations in every region of the world, and sends out press releases on violations to activists worldwide. To subscribe, send the message noted below to the following e-mail address:
<majordomo@igc.apc.org>
Message: subscribe hrwnews

Feminists Against Violence Network (FAVNET)
This group includes human rights activists, legal advocates, torture survivors and concerned citizens. For more information, send an e-mail to:
<favnet@otd.com>

Women.violence
This is an online conference for news, articles, action alerts and discussions focusing on violence against women. To join,
contact:<women.violence@conf.igc.apc.org>

Synergy Gender and Development /ENDA
This organization is based in Dakar, Senegal, and works in partnership with associations, groups and networks active in economics, environment, health, violence and communication for women. Its Web site is bilingual (French and English):
Contact: <http://www.enda. sn/synfev/synfev.htm>

Women's Caucus for Gender Justice in the International Criminal Court
With regional focal points worldwide, the Caucus can be reached at :
P.O. Box 3541
Grand Central Post Office
New York, NY 10163, **USA**
e-mail: <iccwomen@igc.org>

66 RIGHTS OF WOMEN

Reproductive Rights

Each year, more than half a million women (99 percent of them from countries in the Global South) die from causes related to pregnancy and childbirth. Seventy thousand women die from unsafe abortions. Seven million infants die annually because their mothers were not physically ready for childbirth or lacked adequate obstetric care.

These and other grim findings have formed the statistical backbone of a global campaign for women's reproductive rights. They have been presented and debated at nearly every global conference in the 1990s, including the 1994 UN International Conference on Population and Development (ICPD) held in Cairo and the 1995 UN Fourth World Conference on Women (FWCW) held in Beijing. As a result of these debates, women's reproductive rights have finally been recognized as parts of other human rights that are already guaranteed in several international treaties (see box on page 68). These rights include:

- the right to life, liberty, and security;
- the right to be free from gender discrimination;
- the right to health, reproductive health, and family planning;
- the right to modify customary practices that discriminate against women;
- the right to privacy;
- the right to marry and to start a family;
- the right to decide the number and spacing of children;
- the right not to be subject to torture or other cruel, inhuman, or degrading treatment or punishment;
- the right to be free from sexual assault and exploitation;
- the right to enjoy scientific progress and to consent to experimentation.

The recognition of reproductive rights as an integral part of women's human rights was a crucial step forward in the global campaign.

Now activists' focus is on lobbying governments to fulfill the commitments made both when they ratified the international treaties and when they agreed to the documents that came out of the global conferences. Countries must adopt the legal and policy measures necessary to enable women to exercise their reproductive rights. To that end, the international women's rights community is following up on these conferences by working with the UN committees that monitor the main international human rights treaties—the CEDAW Committee, the Human Rights Committee, the

DEVELOPING RIGHTS

Committee on Economic, Social and Cultural Rights and the Committee on the Rights of the Child—as well as other UN groups such as the Commission on the Status of Women. (For more on how the committees monitor the conventions, see Section 1, "Understanding Conventions.") The CEDAW Committee has issued several general recommendations on issues that are closely related to reproductive rights, including violence against women, female genital mutilation, HIV/AIDS, and equality in marriage and family relations (see box below). Furthermore, in July 1997, the CEDAW Committee's chairwoman announced the Committee's intention to issue a General Recommendation on health, including reproductive and sexual health. Such a recommendation would send a powerful and direct message to countries on how they must guarantee women's rights in these areas.

On a national level, activists are preparing for five-year evaluations in 1999 and 2000 that will describe what actions governments have—and have not—taken to implement the ICPD Programme of Action and the FWCW Platform for Action respectively. Reproductive rights groups hope to use these evaluations as an opportunity to air their concerns about their countries' failures to live up to the commitments made at those conferences related to reproductive rights. Because these rights encompass many interrelated aspects of women's health and lives, the most critical concerns at the regional and national levels will certainly vary. In all nations of the world, however, a common concern is to ensure all women's right to attain the highest standard of effective, affordable, and acceptable reproductive health care—free from discrimination, coercion and violence.

RELEVANT DOCUMENTS

Universal Declaration on Human Rights
Articles 2, 3, 5, 16, 25.

International Covenant on Civil and Political Rights Articles 2, 6, 7, 9, 17, 23.

International Covenant on Economic, Social and Cultural Rights Articles 2, 10, 12, 15.

Convention on the Elimination of All Forms of Discrimination Against Women Articles 1, 2, 3, 5, 6, 10, 11, 12, 14, 15, 16.

Convention on the Rights of the Child
Articles 6, 16, 19, 24, 34, 37.

International Convention on the Elimination of All Forms of Racial Discrimination Article 5.

International Conference on Population and Development Programme of Action
See paragraphs 7.1-7.48; 8.19-8.35; 4.1-4.23; 11.1-11.10.

UN Fourth World Conference on Women Platform for Action
See paragraphs 89-130; 259-285.

CEDAW General Recommendation
No. 12 or 19 on Violence Against Women
states that the Committee considers gender-based violence to be a form of gender discrimination, and therefore outlawed by CEDAW.

CEDAW General Recommendation No. 14 on Female Circumcision.

States the Committee's view that appropriate and effective measure must be taken to eradicate female genital mutilation.

CEDAW General Recommendation No. 15 on HIV/AIDS.

Requires states parties to include information on AIDS and its effect on women and recommends certain national-level actions to address such effects.

CEDAW Recommendation No. 21 on Equality in Marriage and Family Relations.

Outlines the Committee's views on the importance of women's basic rights within the family.

CEDAW General Recommendation No. __ on Women's Health (forthcoming).

It is expected that this recommendation will emphasize health-related discrimination that affects women in all stages of their lives, including regarding their reproductive lives, and will recommend certain actions to redress such discrimination in all its forms.

Resources/Contacts

BOOKS

SELECTED PUBLICATIONS
AVAILABLE FROM WOMEN, INK.*

Promoting Reproductive Rights: A Global Mandate *Reed Boland and Anika Rahman*
Focuses on the recognition of reproductive rights at the major UN world conferences of the 1990s, including the declaration of women's rights as human rights and affirmation of the right to access to reproductive health services.
Center for Reproductive Law and Policy, 1997. $10.00

Reproductive Rights in Practice *Anita Hardon and Elizabeth Hayes*
Researchers from eight countries analyze the delivery of family planning services and reveal the extremely low quality of care accessible to women in many countries.
Zed Books, 1997. $22.50

The Right to Reproductive Choice: A Study in International Law *Corinne A.A. Packer*
Presents the underlying rationale for the right to reproductive choice, and defines this right in international law.
Institute for Human Rights, 1996. $32.00

Women of the World: Formal Laws and Policies Affecting Their Reproductive Lives
Reviews the formal laws and policies of Brazil, China, India, Germany, Nigeria and the United States, identifies the factors underlying policy and provides summary statistics.
Center for Reproductive Law and Policy, 1995. $5.00

* Contact information on page 146.

CONTACTS

INTERNATIONAL LEVEL

The Center for Reproductive Law and Policy (CRLP)
120 Wall St., 18th floor, New York, NY 10005, **USA**
Tel: (1-212) 514-5534 Fax: (1-212) 514-5538
E-mail: <info@crlp.org>

International Women's Health Coalition (IWHC)
24 East 21st Street, New York, NY 10010, **USA**
Tel: (1-212) 979-8500 Fax: (1-212) 979-9009
E-mail: <iwhc@iwhc.org>
Web site: <www.iwhc.org>

Development Alternatives with Women for a New Era (DAWN)
c/o University of the S. Pacific, Box 1168, Suva, **FIJI**
Tel: (679) 31-39-00 Fax: (679) 30-14-87
E-mail: <dawn@is.com.fj>
Contact: Claire Slatter

Women's Global Network for Reproductive Rights
NZ Voorburgwal 32, 1012 RZ, Amsterdam, **THE NETHERLANDS**
Tel: (31-20) 620-9672 Fax: (31-20) 622-2450
E-mail: <office@wgnrr.nl>
Contact: Gisela Dütting

REGIONAL/NATIONAL LEVEL

Bangladesh Women's Health Coalition
GPO Box 2295, Dhaka 1000, **BANGLADESH**
Tel: (880-2) 822-876/810-974 Fax: (880-2) 807-969
E-mail: <bwhc@bdonline.com>

Comité Latinoamericano y del Caribe para la Defensa de la Mujer (CLADEM)
Estados Unidos 1295, Oficina #702, Lima 11, **PERU**
Tel/Fax: (51-1) 463-5898
E-mail: <postmast@cladem.org.pe>

Estudio para la Defensa de los Derechos de la Mujer (DEMUS)
Caracas 2624, Lima 11, **PERU**
Tel/Fax: (51-1) 463-1236
E-mail: <demus@amauta.rcp.net.pe>

Federation for Women and Family Planning
ul. Franciszkanska 18/20 00-205, Warsaw, **POLAND**
Tel: (48-22) 635-43-76 Fax: (48-22) 635-47-91
E-mail: <polfedwo@waw.pdi.net>

International Federation of Women Lawyers
Mucia Off Ngong Road, P.O. Box 46324, Nairobi, **KENYA**
Tel: (254-2) 71-71-69/71-18-53/71-46-29
Fax: (254-2) 71-68-40/71-12-87
E-mail: <Fida-Kenya@Africaonline.co.ke>

Latin American and Caribbean Women's Health Network
Casilla Postal 50610, Santiago 1, **CHILE**
Tel: (56-2) 634-9827 Fax: (56-2) 634-7101
E-mail: <rslmac@mail.bellsouth.cl>
Web site: <www.infoera.cl/red_de_salud>

Women's Health Project
University of Witswatersrand, P.O. Box 1038, Johannesburg 2000, **SOUTH AFRICA**
Tel: (27-11) 489-9917 Fax: (27-11) 489-9922
E-mail: <womenhp@sn.apc.org>

Environmental

MAKING THE CONNECTION BETWEEN HUMAN RIGHTS AND ENVIRONMENTAL RIGHTS

The health of the individual cannot be separated from the health of the environment. Whereas a healthy environment is advantageous for sustaining life, a toxic environment endangers life. And that threat constitutes a violation of our fundamental right to the highest attainable standard of physical and mental health.

All women have the right to bear children. But pollutants in the air we breathe, in the water we drink and the food we eat harm our reproductive systems and thus infringe on our right to bear children and start a family.

We have the right to live harmoniously in nature. But if we must tell our children not to play in streams because they are contaminated, if eating fish from those streams or foodstuffs grown in soil irrigated by those streams will sicken us, or if the atmosphere carries noxious elements, then our right to live cooperatively with the natural environment has been violated.

We have the right to develop as human beings to our fullest capacity. If pollutants in our air, water or food imperil the developing fetus or child, altering the way in which our children will experience joy, human connection and community, then not only has our right to our own humanity been compromised but humanity itself becomes endangered as well.

EXISTING AGREEMENTS AND DECLARATIONS

Agenda 21, the document resulting from the 1992 Earth Summit (known officially as the UN Conference on Environment and Development, or UNCED) in Rio de Janeiro, states that human beings are at the centre of concerns for sustainable development and that they are entitled to a healthy and productive life in harmony with nature (Principle 1). It further affirms that the right to development must be fulfilled so as to equitably meet environmental needs of present and future generations (Principle 3).

Rights

In order to carry out that right to development, the document asserts that states should discourage or prevent the relocation and transfer to other states of any activities and substances that cause severe environmental degradation or are found to be harmful to human health. (Principle 14).

Agenda 21 acknowledges how critical it is that states recognize the fundamental interconnections between health and environment. Only then can they make efficient use of resources within the carrying capacity of ecosystems. They must further be called upon to provide all people, in particular those belonging to vulnerable and disadvantaged groups, with equal opportunities for a healthy, safe and productive life in harmony with nature.

The document further commits to providing adequate and integrated environmental infrastructure facilities in all settlements as soon as possible, with a view to improving health by ensuring access for all people to sufficient, continuous and safe freshwater facilities, and to sanitation, drainage and waste disposal, with a special emphasis on providing facilities to segments of the population living in poverty.

The Platform for Action and Beijing Declaration from the 1995 Fourth UN World Conference on Women reaffirm the integration of the basic right to health as fundamentally integrated with the right to environmental health. The document calls for a reduction of environmental hazards that pose a growing threat to health, especially in poor regions and communities, and calls for reporting on women's health risks related to the environment in monitoring implementation of Agenda 21.

Finally, the Beijing declarations propose the formulation of special policies, programmes and legislation to alleviate and eliminate environmental and occupational health hazards associated with work in the home, in the workplace and elsewhere, with special attention given to pregnant and lactating women.

Resources/Contacts

BOOKS

SELECTED PUBLICATIONS
AVAILABLE FROM WOMEN, INK.*

Ecofeminism
Marie Mies and Vandana Shiva
Weaves together women's perspectives worldwide into a collective definition of ecofeminism and women's right to environmental health, and redefines sustainable development.
Zed Books, 1993. $19.95

Ecofeminism: Women, Culture, Nature
Katen J. Warren (Ed.)
Explores the concerns that have motivated ecofeminism as a grassroots, women-initiated movement around the globe.
Indiana University Press, 1997. $24.95

Empowerment: Towards Sustainable Development
Naresh Singh and Vangile Titi (Eds.)
Overviews empowerment methods and challenges, examines education as an empowerment tool for women.
Zed Books, 1995. $22.50

Gender and Sustainable Development
Ana Maria Brasileiro (Ed.)
Gives practical examples—including capacity-building around women's environmental rights—of how women throughout Latin America and the Caribbean have organized to integrate the concept of gender-sensitive sustainable development into all development planning and projects.
UNIFEM, 1997. $7.95

Women and Sustainable Development in Africa *Valentine Udoh James (Ed.)*
Argues for the full integration of women into the planning, construction, and implementation of development schemes in Africa, for these to be both successful and sustainable.
Praeger Publishers, 1995. $18.95

***Contact information on page 146.**

CONTACTS

INTERNATIONAL
Women's Environment and Development Organization (WEDO)
355 Lexington Avenue, Third Floor
New York, NY 10017-6603, **USA**
Tel: (1-212) 973-0325 Fax: (1-212) 973-0335
E-mail: ‹wedo@igc.apc.org›
Web site: ‹http://www.wedo.org›
Contact: Anita Nayar or Mim Kelber

Woman and Earth Global Eco-Network
467 Central Park West, Suite 7F
New York, NY 10025, **USA**
Tel: (1-212) 866-8130 Fax: (1-516) 368-1652
E-mail: ‹womearth@dorsai.org›
Web site: ‹http://www.dorsai.org/~womearth›
Contact: Tatyana Mamanova and Carmella Mildred Didio

REGIONAL
Africa
Network of African Rural Women
No. 7 Awosika Crescent, Ilapo Estate,
P.M.B. 809, Akure, Ondo State, **NIGERIA**
Tel: (234-34) 23-19-45 Fax: (234-34) 23-16-33
Contact: Chief Bisi Ogunleye

Asia-Pacific
Asian Indigenous Women's Network
P.O. Box 7691 Garcom Baguio
Dapo 1300, Domestic Road, Pasay City
THE PHILIPPINES
Tel: (63-74) 442-5347 Fax: (63-74) 442-5205
E-mail: ‹vicorpuz@phil.gn.apc.org›
Contact: Victoria Tauli-Corpuz

Ecowoman
c/o SPACHEE
Box 16737, GPO Suva, **FIJI**
Tel: (679) 312-271 Fax: (679) 303-053
E-mail: ‹morris_ch@usp.ac.fj›
Contact: Cherie Morris
Web site: ‹www.wigsat.org/ofan/activities/ecowoman›

Europe
Association of Women of the Mediterranean Region
P.O. Box 320, Limassol 3603, **CYPRUS**
Tel: (357-5) 37-24-97 Fax: (357-5) 36-84-57
E-mail: ‹npourou@anet.com.cy›
Contact: Ninetta Pourou-Kazantzis

Women in Europe for a Common Future
P.O. Box 12111, 3501 AC Utrecht
THE NETHERLANDS
Tel: (31-30) 213-0300 Fax: (31-30) 234-0878
E-mail: ‹wecf@antenna.nl›
Contact: Sacscha Gabizon

Women's Environment Network
Aberdeen Studios, 22 Highbury Grove
London N5 2EA, **UNITED KINGDOM**
Tel: (44-171) 354-8823 Fax: (44-171) 354-0464
Contact: Clare Flenley

Eastern Europe/Countries in Transition
MAMA-86
Michailovska Str. 22-A, Kiev 25001,
UKRAINE
Tel: (380-44) 228-3101 Fax: (380-44) 229-5514
E-mail: ‹mama-86@gluk.apc.org›
Contact: Anna Onisimova

Latin America-Caribbean
REDEH-Network in Defense of Humankind
Rua Alvaro Alvim, 21, 16th Floor
Rio de Janeiro-Centro, **BRAZIL**
Tel: (55-21) 262-1704 Fax: (55-21) 262-6454
E-mail: ‹thaisc@ax.apc.org›
Contact: Thais Corral

Guyana Society for the Protection and Preservation of the Environment
97 Fourth Avenue, Barica
Essequibo River, **GUYANA**
Tel: (592) 52409
Contact: Judith Davi

Middle East
ENDA
6, rue Imam Termadi, Ksar Said 11
2009 **TUNISIA**
Tel: (216-1) 51-52-17 Fax: (216-1) 58-27-83
E-mail: ‹endarab@gn.apc.org›
Contact: Essma Ben Hamida

North America
Women's Network on Health and the Environment
4 Walmer Rd., Apt 1006, Toronto
ONT M5R 2X5, **CANADA**
Tel: (1-416) 960-4944 Fax: (1-416) 531-6214
Contact: Dorothy Goldin-Rosenberg

Resource Center for Community Health and Environmental Justice
P.O. Box 615, Kyle, TX 78640, **USA**
Tel: (1-512) 268-2220 Fax: (1-512) 268-1557

Women with Disabilities

WOMEN WITH DISABILITIES DEMAND THEIR RIGHTS

At the International Leadership Forum for Women with Disabilities held in June, 1997, 614 women from 82 countries, encouraged by the emerging strength and empowerment of women and girls with disabilities, issued a powerful statement that included the following:

"We believe that several concrete actions and considerations must occur regarding (additions to) UN conventions and policies, specifically: the Convention on the Elimination of All Forms of Discrimination Against Women (CEDAW); the Convention on the Rights of the Child (CRC); the Standard Rules on the Equalization of Opportunities for Persons with Disabilities, and the Beijing Platform for Action."

"I've been taking self-defense classes and I feel more independent now."

violence against disabled women and girls as a critical health and human rights issue. Legal enforcement of assault and sexual abuse laws should be strengthened, including severe punishment of offenders, and support for victims throughout the justice system."

"We cannot accept that family members, paid and volunteer care givers, institutional staff, police and even friends are humiliating, assaulting, raping, exploiting, neglecting, forcibly isolating, withholding assistance, medical care or supports, abandoning, disposing of, putting out to beg, selling and even killing women and girls with disabilities at alarming rates. We request that the UN Special Rapporteur on Violence Against Women address violence against women and girls with disabilities as a pressing issue, in full cooperation with women with disabilities and their organizations."

•**Human Rights and Violence:** "Disabled women and girls must be heard clearly in all debates and policies concerning genetic engineering, bioethics, prosthetic design and human implants (including cochlear implants), abortion on the grounds of disability, assisted suicide, euthanasia and all eugenic practices. We urge that international and national governmental and non-governmental organizations recognize the high rate of

•**Education:** "We demand effective access to education and employment as the primary tools for fighting poverty. We urge that education be used as the primary key for girls and women to be able to lead integrated and participatory lives in our communities. We urge that both parents and teachers of girls with disabilities receive further training in order that the quality of overall education be raised."

- **Employment:** "We demand that women with disabilities be afforded full support to pursue their ambitions and skills development regarding the use of their capabilities. We urge that women with disabilities be encouraged to establish microenterprises. Banks should recognize the multiple value of giving loans to women's business enterprises."

- **Health Care:** "Women with disabilities do not have equal access to quality health care. Disabled women are dying prematurely as a result of not getting the care they need. Therefore, we demand:
  - That women be allowed to take power and control over their own health care, including having the choice of what medical tests and treatments they wish to have.
  - That national health policies and bureaucracies be accountable for improving the access, availability and affordability of high quality, culturally appropriate health care for women and girls with disabilities.
  - That schools for health professionals make it possible for students with disabilities to be trained, and include adequate training to all students on the needs of women and girls with disabilities.
  - The development of adaptive equipment, appropriate to local conditions.
  - That women with disabilities be trained as leaders in research in disabled women's health care needs.
  - That quality field-based health services be provided for disabled women and girls in war-torn areas."

- **Sexuality:** "We urge that women have a safe and private place to discuss with each other their sexual lives, desires, hopes and needs. Furthermore, we urge that women and girls receive accurate information about sexuality, including training to publicize the fact that all disabled women are sexual and sexy and can give and receive love in a variety of ways. Disabled women should be trained to work in women's health services and to inform disabled women and girls of their reproductive rights, including training as sex educators, family planners, and leaders in research on disabled women's sexuality."

- **Media Portrayals and Access to Communication Technology:** "We demand the inclusion of positive images of women and girls with disabilities in the media. These portrayals must be sensitive and life-enhancing. Furthermore, all technical methods of communication should be designed for universal use by both disabled and able-bodied persons. The communications and information needs of disabled women who are poor and have not received an education should be given the highest priority."

- **Public Transportation:** "We demand that all public forms of transportation, including buses, trains, planes and subways, be fully accessible to women and girls with disabilities, to enable us to fully participate in the life of our communities."

- **UN Conventions:** "We urge the United Nations and its Member States to implement all existing conventions concerning disabled women and girls. We also urge immediate action regarding making existing conventions accessible to all people with disabilities, using easy-to-read language, large print, braille and other accessible formats and local languages as needed."

"Together we are strong!"

Resources/Contacts

BOOKS

SELECTED PUBLICATIONS
AVAILABLE FROM WOMEN, INK.*

Across Borders: Women with Disabilities Working Together *Diane Driedger, Irene Feika and Eileen Girón*
Shows how women with disabilities have fought for—and achieved—full participation in society by organizing self-help groups, asserting their rights within their country's disabilities movement and building partnerships with other groups around the world.
Gynergy Books, 1996. $14.95

Gender and Disability: Women's Experiences in the Middle East *Lina Abu-Habib*
Studying the lives of women with disabilities in the Middle East region makes it very clear how gender and disability interact as factors of social differentiation.
Oxfam, 1997. $9.95

Loud, Proud and Passionate: Including Women with Disabilities in International Development Programmes
With a special focus on women in Africa, Latin America, the Caribbean, and Europe, this book describes projects organized by, and for, women with disabilities to improve opportunities for income generation, education, health, and full participation in communities.
Mobility International, 1997. $19.95

* Contact information on page 146.

CONTACTS

Disabled Peoples' International (DPI)
P.O. Box 267, 00171
Helsinki, **FINLAND**
Tel: (358-9) 160-3880 Fax: (358-9) 160-4312

International Council on Disability (ICOD)
P.O. Box 3488, 11471
Riyadh, **SAUDI ARABIA**
Tel: (966-1) 488-2917 Fax: (966-1) 488-8260

Rehabilitation International
25 East 21st Street,
New York, NY 10010 **USA**
Tel: (1-212) 420-1500 Fax: (1-212) 505-0871

International League of Societies for Persons with Mental Handicap (ILSMH)
Gal. de la Toison d'Or, 20 Chausee,
D'Izelles, 393-35
Brussels B-1050, **BELGIUM**
Tel: (32-2) 502-7734 Fax: (32-2) 502-2846

Psychiatric Survivors
P.O. Box 78-7172, Grey Lynn,
Auckland, **NEW ZEALAND**
Tel: (64-9) 376-0041 Fax: (64-9) 360-2180

World Blind Union
224 Great Portland Street,
London WIN 6AA,
UNITED KINGDOM
Tel: (44-171) 388-1266 Fax: (44-171)383-0508

World Federation of the Deaf
P.O. Box 65, SF-004401
Helsinki, **FINLAND**
Tel: (358-9) 580-3100 Fax: (358-9) 580-3770

ONLINE CONTACTS

Society for All Network
E-mail: ‹outi.aalto@stakes.fi›
Web site: ‹http://www.stakes.fi/sfa›

European Network of Women with Disabilities
E-mail: ‹outi.aalto@stakes.fi›
Web site: ‹http://www.disweb.org›

For information on the International Leadership Forum for Women with Disabilities
Project Director: Kathy Martinez,
World Institute on Disability,
510 16th St. Oakland, CA 944612, USA
Tel: (1-510) 251-4326 Fax: (1-510) 208-9494
E-mail: ‹kathy@wid.org›

FACT

There are more than 300 million women with disabilities in the world. In many societies they are consigned to the margins—not admitted to schools, rejected by employers, denied access to health care.

Sexual Orientation Rights

BOOKS

AVAILABLE FROM WOMEN, INK.*

Unspoken Rules: Sexual Orientation and Women's Rights
Rachel Rosenbloom (Ed.)
The 30 country reports in this unique volume document human rights violations based on sexual orientation, touching on a whole host of legal, cultural, social and economic issues and showing how women's rights and lesbian rights are linked in substantive ways.
Cassell, 1996. $21.95

* Contact information on page 146.

CONTACTS

International Gay and Lesbian Human Rights Commission
1360 Mission St., Ste 200
San Francisco, CA 94103
USA
Tel: (1-415) 255-8680
Fax: (1-415) 255-8662
E-mail: <sydney@iglhrc.org>
Contact: Sydney Levy

Amnesty International
1 Easton Street
London WC1X-8DJ
UNITED KINGDOM
Tel: (44-171) 413-5911
Fax: (44-171) 956-1157
E-mail: <amnesty@gn.apc.org>
Contact: Edna Aquino

STRATEGIES TO BRING INTERNATIONAL ATTENTION TO GAY AND LESBIAN HUMAN RIGHTS

Discrimination experienced by lesbians and gay men as a result of their sexual orientation is not explicitly recognized by any human rights document. Consequently, activists have had to rely on a combination of strategies to bring international attention to the rights of the gay community.

Regionally and internationally, human rights activists have been working for re-interpretations of existing human rights documents. In 1981 they won a landmark decision when the European Court of Human Rights found that the right to privacy as described in the European Human Rights Convention prevented the criminalization of sexual orientation by European countries.

Activists had to wait more than ten years for the UN Commission on Human Rights, which oversees the International Covenant on Civil and Political Rights (ICCPR), to reach another historic decision. In 1993, the committee held that the prohibition against sex discrimination in the ICCPR included discrimination on the basis of sexual orientation.

These watershed decisions notwithstanding, lesbian and gay activists have been frustrated in their attempts to create international momentum. At the 1993 World Conference on Human Rights in Vienna, attention was drawn to the need to recognize sexual rights as human rights, although no reference to sexual rights was made in the official conference declaration. Two years later, "sexual orientation" was mentioned four times in the draft Beijing Platform for Action that was to be debated and adopted at the Fourth World Conference on Women. Unfortunately, in the closing session of the conference, all four references were deleted. However, several states did issue supplementary statements indicating that they interpreted the term "sexual rights" and some other human rights laws that were explicitly against discrimination to include sexual orientation.

There are some promising signs that indicate that some countries are beginning to recognize that discrimination against anyone on the basis of sexual orientation is a violation of their human rights. For example, in the new South African Constitution, discrimination on the basis of sexual orientation is explicitly recognized as a violation of a citizen's human rights under the law.

76 RIGHTS OF WOMEN

4
Taking Action

IN THIS SECTION

Converting Words into Action
- A Country Manual
- A Tribunal: Making Women's Voices Heard
- Information Tools: Building Human Rights Communities

Converting Words into Action

INTRODUCTION

In communities worldwide, from Cairo to Calcutta, New York to Nairobi, women are moving into the public arena in the follow-up to the 1995 Beijing world meetings. We are forging new styles of leadership, developing new strategies to link the global with the local, and searching for new tools with which to leverage change and to champion issues.

With each step, there is new knowledge and experience gained. For example, at a UN meeting to review reports from countries who had ratified CEDAW, an NGO delegation from one of the reporting countries invited a noted journalist from their home country to be present at their presentation of a "Shadow Report". The journalist followed up with a feature article which appeared the next day on the front page of a major daily newspaper in the home country. It focused public attention on these issues as never before, and forced the government to take notice!

For a variety of reasons, information about international conventions has had very limited circulation. Lawyers frequently have only a passing understanding of international law; advocates on specific issues are frequently not even aware that international conventions could be of use to them; and government officials with a responsibility for gender issue many times may have heard of international conventions, but have had little opportunity to explore what the practical implications might be.

Only in recent years have women really begun to focus on ways to use global policy and international conventions to create change at the national level.

THREE ACTIONS

Conventions are a tool and, like any tool, their power lies in their use. The following chapter presents three different approaches to working with international conventions. They are:

1. Creating a Country Manual, or guide to international conventions and national laws, to increase access to information about laws and conventions within a country or community. Such a manual could act as an effective tool within a larger campaign strategy.

2. Holding a Tribunal, or a public forum where individuals give testimony to a panel of legal experts on human rights violations that had previously been invisible or ignored in the legal system.

3. Using Information Tools, particularly activities made possible through the use of new information technology. This section focuses on ways of sharing, recording and producing human rights information, and of reaching out to online human rights communities.

A Country Manual

A GUIDE TO WOMEN'S HUMAN RIGHTS THAT ARE PROTECTED BY UN CONVENTIONS

The country manual concept described in this section is intended as a way to make international conventions known, accessible, and real to women working to promote change at the community and country level. The basic core of a country manual is the bringing together of international conventions with the laws of the country.

Ideally, and in order to a create an action tool, other ingredients would also be added, such as:

a. a directory, complete with name, address, phone, and fax of key groups (e.g. lawyers, journalists, researchers, government personnel, networks, national activist groups, etc.)
b. an overview of the issue
c. relevant facts and figures.

BUILDING A COALITION

To create a country manual requires the combined expertise of individuals and groups in different sectors. In fact, the process of pulling the information together can be an integral part of a coalition-building process that is absolutely essential for effective action. In the end, what is created is a resource that can be shared widely among groups and individual activists, and used as a tool within a larger campaign to advance and secure women's rights. In the process, what is created is a stronger coalition based on each group feeling valued for its contribution, with a greater sense of ownership of the conventions. The proposed country manual is adaptable to each specific country. It can be developed around one issue and convention, or around several issues and conventions.

START SMALL, THINK BIG, ACT NOW...

The process presented in the following pages is a single issue approach. Working with international conventions can be overwhelming initially and few groups are in a position to work on all issues at once. But imagine what might happen if several groups, each working on their own issue, collaborated together. The result might be a country manual of UN conventions, national laws and local realities that all groups could use as an advocacy tool.

TAKING ACTION **79**

CREATING A COUNTRY MANUAL

WHY CREATE A COUNTRY MANUAL?

> *I'm learning how to read so I can read about my rights*
>
> Kamla Bhasin,
> writer, researcher, trainer
> in India

A country manual presents an overview of an issue or issues and explains which international conventions and local laws are relevant to it. It shows where your country stands with regard to ratification and reservations—that is, how the government has positioned itself on the particular issue—and provides contact information for the government ministry responsible for its implementation, the international bodies responsible for monitoring, and local, regional and international networks working on the issue.

Creating a country manual not only provides you with a tool that can be used to further your work around women's human rights. It also offers your group a number of other opportunities, which include: educating the group about the selected issue(s) and the related conventions and laws; getting up-to-date with the current thinking around women's human rights; coalition-building with other organizations; developing contacts with experts; and opening up talks with the government around the issue.

SOME POINTS TO KEEP IN MIND

1. Keep the language simple and straightforward. The intent is to give your colleagues an advocacy tool that they can easily use in various public fora.

2. Leave wide margins so that people can write notes by those portions of the manual that they find of most interest.

3. Take care in citing your sources accurately.

4. Use illustrations wherever possible. They can enliven a page and catch people's attention.

5. Use examples from your own country or region liberally throughout as this is an important way of making the conventions real and concrete for your home situation.

6. Consider using "attention-getter" pages of quotes, slogans, images or any combination thereof that brings the issue alive

7. Use the guide as an opportunity to strengthen your coalition. Identify groups who can contribute. In the end this builds ownership and enhances its usefulness.

80 RIGHTS OF WOMEN

CREATING A COUNTRY MANUAL

A BASIC OUTLINE FOR A COUNTRY MANUAL

A basic outline for a country manual should contain the following ingredients to make it a more effective advocacy and community awareness tool. You will probably have more suggestions.

> "I'm learning how to count so that I can keep an account of my own rights."
>
> Kamla Bhasin,
> writer, researcher, trainer in India

1. **An international, regional and national overview of the issue**. You may wish to use and adapt the international overviews presented in *Rights of Women*, if appropriate for your issue.

2. **A global-local matching page** in which the international convention is matched with the national law to which it relates. You will need to take the key paragraphs or clauses of the conventions and find the corresponding paragraphs or points in your national legislation.

3. **An overview** of what the country's status is regarding the convention.

4. **Some key points or clauses of a convention** that are considered most critical for the issue you are working on matched with the government ministry responsible for implementation.

5. **A directory of national organizations** working on the issue with name and contact information (address, phone, fax, e-mail, etc.) List both those in favor of change as well as those opposing it. This directory could be added to by including the names and contact information for journalists, lawyers and legal aid groups, human rights organizations, teachers, researchers, and other concerned professionals working on the issue.

6. **A listing of international and regional organizations and networks,** both UN, governmental and non-governmental, working on the specific issue.

7. **A facts and figures page** presenting information deemed vital for presenting the scope or severity of the problem you are working on—ideally presenting both international or regional data matched with national or local data.

8. **A list of selected readings,** key periodicals or a reading list identifying sources for more in-depth information that would be important reading for anyone wanting to use the international conventions to promote change at country level.

TAKING ACTION **81**

HOW TO PUT YOUR

START HERE

1. Decide on your issue (or right). Review Section 2 of this manual to find which conventions are relevant. Prepare Worksheet #1: "Linking an Issue to the Conventions." (p. 87).

2. Fill out Worksheet #2 "Convention Profile": To find the information for your country, use the Ratification Charts in Section 5, (pp. 126-135) and the "Information Finder" (p. 91).

3. Review Worksheet #3 "Questions to Ask about Each Convention" (p. 89), and discuss whether any other questions should be asked. Additional questions might include those that are specific to a convention or the answers to which would offer a better understanding of your country's position concerning this convention.

7. Make a work plan identifying what information you need to gather, and where you can get it. (See Handout 2: "Information Finder", p. 91). This step can be particularly useful as part of a coalition-building process with other groups. The information-gathering step includes research on your country's stand on specific conventions relevant to the issues on which you are working. If your country has ratified the convention(s), find out whether or not it had reservations, and if so, what the specific reservations were. Identifying the reservations makes it possible to begin mapping the issues that are most problematic for your government to accept.

"Well, here's our workplan. Now who can we get to help us?"

"I'm sure other women's groups will help us. And I know several lawyers who work on human rights issues."

8. Develop a production plan. Decide whether or not you will use a computer and if you will get information from the Internet. Included within your production plan should be a page layout for your publication.

82 RIGHTS OF WOMEN

COUNTRY MANUAL TOGETHER

4. Use these questions as part of an overall analysis of the issue. Discuss how the convention(s) can be used as part of overall campaign on issue.

5. Discuss who might use the manual. Decide who your primary audience is and who might be your secondary audiences. Review and make additions to the Handout 1: "Audience Profile Chart" (p. 90) which shows how each group benefits and what each group could contribute.

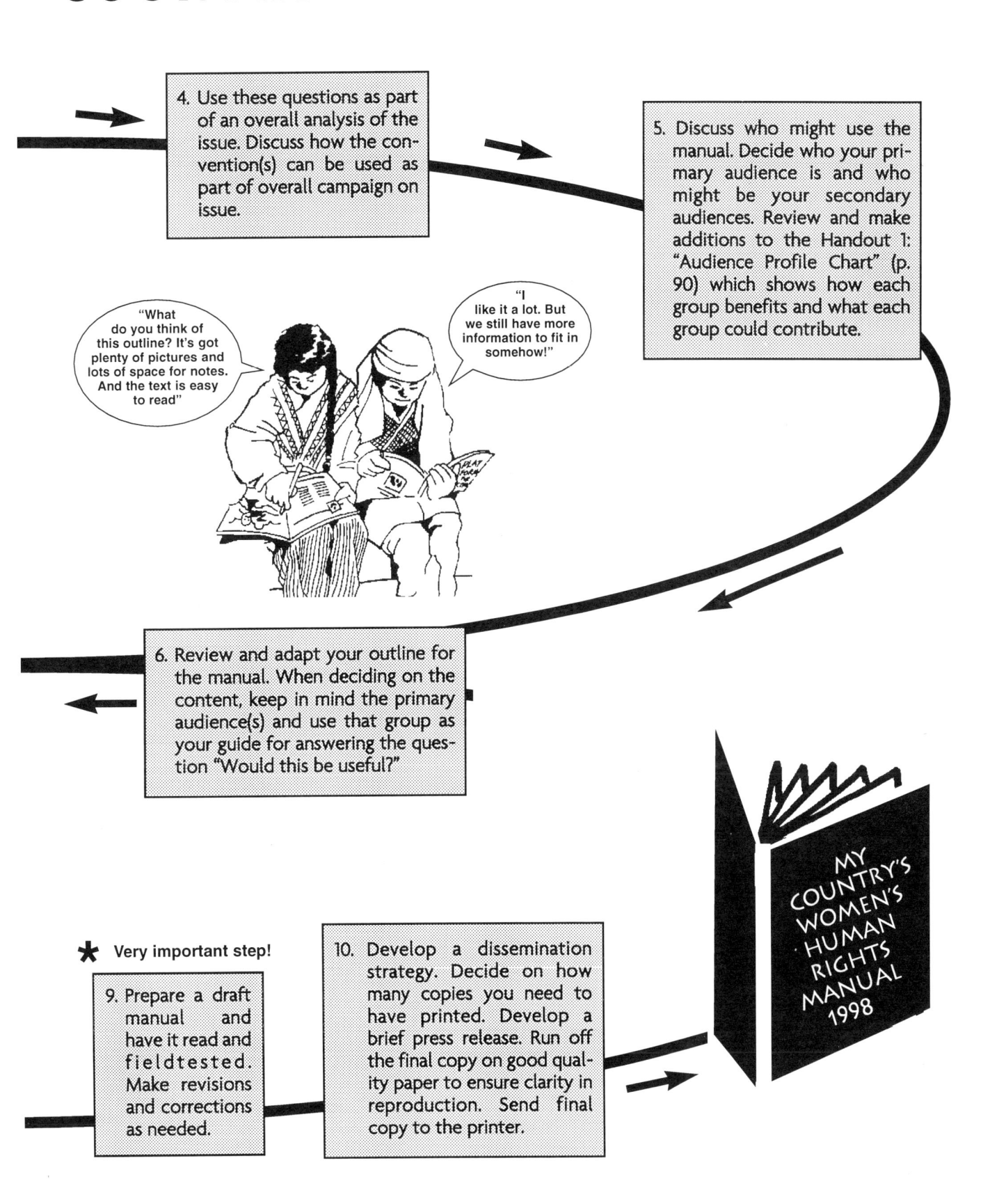

"What do you think of this outline? It's got plenty of pictures and lots of space for notes. And the text is easy to read"

"I like it a lot. But we still have more information to fit in somehow!"

6. Review and adapt your outline for the manual. When deciding on the content, keep in mind the primary audience(s) and use that group as your guide for answering the question "Would this be useful?"

* Very important step!

9. Prepare a draft manual and have it read and **fieldtested**. Make revisions and corrections as needed.

10. Develop a dissemination strategy. Decide on how many copies you need to have printed. Develop a brief press release. Run off the final copy on good quality paper to ensure clarity in reproduction. Send final copy to the printer.

MY COUNTRY'S WOMEN'S HUMAN RIGHTS MANUAL 1998

CREATING A COUNTRY MANUAL

DIFFERENT STROKES FOR DIFFERENT FOLKS...

Once you have gathered all the information you need for your manual, think of other ways in which you could put the information together. Different formats are useful for different uses. For instance, a booklet brings everything together in one place and should probably be the main publication. A pamphlet makes a good handout however, and for those with computers, a computer disk containing the text would be invaluable. Below you will find nine suggested ways to present your findings, with a description of each format on the page opposite.

1. COUNTRY MANUAL ON WOMEN'S RIGHTS
2. TRAINING GUIDE for WOMEN'S HUMAN RIGHTS
3. SELECTED RECOMMENDATIONS FROM COUNTRY MANUAL ON WOMEN'S RIGHTS
4. RIGHTS OF WOMEN / INTERNATIONAL CONVENTIONS (Education, Employment, Marriage, Refugees, Sexual Expl., Torture)
5. YOUR RIGHTS IN A NUTSHELL!
6. WOMEN'S RIGHTS ARE HUMAN RIGHTS!
7. WOMEN'S RIGHTS ARE HUMAN RIGHTS
8. "Do you know what your rights are?"
9. COUNTRY MANUAL DISK

84 RIGHTS OF WOMEN

CREATING A COUNTRY MANUAL

BRIEF DESCRIPTION OF SUGGESTED FORMATS FOR COUNTRY MANUAL ILLUSTRATED ON OPPOSITE PAGE

1. A booklet containing the full text version of the country manual. It should be in a handy size, not too big, for use by activists, community groups, agencies, lawyers, libraries, resource centres, and for women to carry around!

2. A Training Guide for Women's Human Rights, with participatory training activities and simulation games of various kinds for informing individuals, community groups and agencies about the rights that women have.

3. A book of selected recommendations from the country manual would make a great handout, especially for government people and community workers.

4. A country manual wall chart that lists the various rights of women, and the conventions that established these rights. Other wall charts could show the different but complementary roles of the government and the civil sector in implementing these rights.

5. A pocket size brochure summarizing key points of the country manual would be ideal as a handout, for desk reference and for speaking engagements.

6. A poster visualizing the rights that women have as embodied in the conventions outlined in the country manual.

7. A postcard series, perhaps a different postcard for each of the conventions outlined in the country manual, or a series focusing on the various rights covered in the conventions.

8. A series of radio programmes on cassette developed around the rights covered in the conventions in the country manual.

9. A computer disk containing the text of the country manual would be very useful for those groups with computers who could include parts of the text in their own publications, send all or part of the text off to other groups via e-mail, place it on their Web-site on the Internet, etc.

How to Use the Worksheets

The following worksheets and handouts are designed to stimulate your thinking, provide easy access to information found in disparate places, and/or suggest some practical first steps to get you on your way to creating a country manual. Feel free to adapt and create new worksheets as the need arises!

WORKSHEET 1. (P. 87)
"Linking an Issue to the Conventions"

The first step is to identify your issue and determine if there are any particular points within it that are of special interest to your group. For example, you may be interested in pressuring your government to develop new curriculum materials for primary schools in the area of science and technology for girls. The broad issue, then, is education, and the specific points are curriculum development and science and technology education.

Next, find your convention(s) by turning to Chapter 2. You will note that we have provided information not only on conventions but also on the policy declarations relevant to the topic. In the second column, write in the numbers of the paragraphs that relate to your specific concerns. This is important because in presenting your case you will want to be able to state not only which convention but which paragraphs, serve to support your claim.

The information necessary to complete the remaining columns can all be found by referring to the Information Finder Handout. It is vital to know where your country stands concerning the issue to then be able to hold your government accountable.

WORKSHEET 2. (P. 88)
"Convention Profile"

This chart, when completed, offers an overview of where your country stands on all the international human rights conventions of particular relevance to women. It can be filled out by using the ratification charts beginning on p. 127 and the "Information Finder" (p. 91). It is a great advocacy tool to use as a handout to groups of diverse interests to give a quick overview of where your country stands concerning women's human rights issues and could be blown up to poster size.

WORKSHEET 3. (P. 89)
"Questions to Ask about Each Convention"

The questions on this page enable you to explore in more depth your country's position with respect to the particular human rights issue protected by the convention(s). You will probably be able to answer many of the questions based on your own analysis and experience in working with the issue (i.e. what customs or traditions make it difficult to observe the rights covered). Other answers are in this manual and can be accessed by using the "Information Finder" handout (p. 91) and some may require input from a friendly lawyer (what laws must be changed) or other research.

HANDOUT 1. (P. 90)
"Audience Profile Chart"

Increasing people's access to information in order to enable them to use international conventions for advocacy on behalf of women is a primary purpose of a country manual. Understanding who will use the manual is an important consideration, therefore, in deciding the format, language and approach you take. Use this chart to stimulate thinking about this and to suggest who might be natural collaborators in a production of this kind.

HANDOUT 2. (P. 91)
"Information Finder"

This sheet is organized by what information you are looking for, and where, in this manual or elsewhere, to find it. It is intended to provide a shortcut to your research process and to therefore serve as a timesaver.

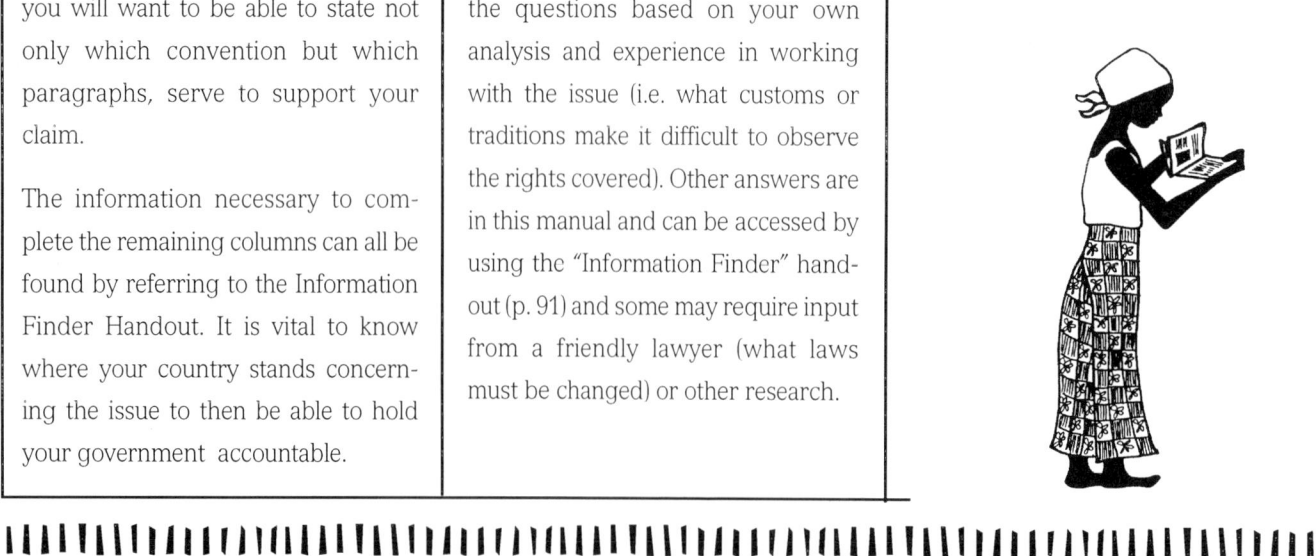

Worksheet 1
"Linking an Issue to the Conventions"

Country: _____

The issue is: _____

Our rights: _____
_____

Country Report Available Y/N				
International Monitoring/Complaint Procedure				
Reservations				
Ratified Y/N				
Relevant Paragraphs				
Relevant Conventions				

TAKING ACTION **87**

Worksheet 2
"Convention Profile: Where Does My Country Stand?"

Country: _____

Convention	Year in Force	Ratified Y/N	Reservations Y/N
Universal Declaration of Human Rights (UDHR)	1948		
International Covenant on Civil and Political Rights (ICCPR)	1966		
Optional Protocol on Civil and Political Rights (OPICCPR)	1966		
International Covenant on Economic, Social and Cultural Rights (ICESCR)	1966		
Convention on the Elimination of All Forms of Discrimination Against Women (CEDAW)	1981		
International Convention on the Elimination of All Forms of Racial Discrimination (ICERD)	1965		
Convention on the Rights of the Child (CRC)	1989		
Convention Against Discrimination in Education (CDE)	1960		
Equal Remuneration Convention (ERC)	1953		
Maternity Protection Convention (MPC)	1955		
Discrimination (Employment and Occupation) Convention (DC)	1960		
Workers with Family Responsibilities Convention (WFRC)	1983		
Home Work Convention (HWC) (not yet entered into force)			
Convention on the Nationality of Married Women (CNMW)	1957		
Convention on Consent to Marriage, Minimum Age for Marriage and Registration of Marriages (CCM)	1962		
Convention Relating to the Status of Refugees (CRSR)	1951		
Convention for the Suppression of Traffic in Persons and of the Exploitation of the Prostitution of Others (CSTPEP)	1949		
Supplementary Convention on the Abolition of Slavery, the Slave Trade, and Institutions and Practices Similar to Slavery (SCAS)	1956		
Convention Against Torture and Other Cruel, Inhuman or Degrading Treatment or Punishment (CAT)	1984		
Protocol Relating to the Status of Refugees	1967		
Convention on the Political Rights of Women (CPRW)	1953		
Convention Relating to the Status of Stateless Persons (CSSP)	1954		
Convention on the Reduction of Statelessness (CRS)	1961		

Worksheet 3
"Questions To Ask About Each Convention"

(You can photocopy this page if you are working on more than one convention.)

CONVENTION: _____

HAS THIS CONVENTION BEEN RATIFIED?   ☐ YES   ☐ NO

IF YES:
Which laws must be (or have been) changed? _____
_____
_____

Which provisions are especially important for women? _____
_____
_____

What customs or traditions make it difficult to observe the rights covered? _____
_____
_____

If reservations have been submitted, what are they and why? _____
_____
_____

Which government ministry monitors the status of this convention? _____

Which government ministry is responsible for implementation? _____

Do the periodic reports submitted to the UN reflect the real situation in the country? _____

Are reports available to the public and, if so, where can they be obtained? _____
_____

If NO:
Which government body must ratify and when do they vote? _____
_____

What are the reasons for not ratifying? _____
_____

TAKING ACTION

Handout 1
"Audience Profile Chart"

Audience Type	How the Manual Benefits Them	What They Can Contribute
1. Women's Groups/ Individual Women's Rights Activists	1. Provides issue overview and description of relevant laws written in accessible language • Adds weight and substance to campaigns to improve status of women since can reference conventions country has already agreed to • Increases collaboration opportunities since key groups with different expertise identified • Builds bonds with groups for later collective action • Decreases reliance on needing a lawyer to pull the information together • Organizes contact information so that it can be used repeatedly • Gives point of entry for talking knowledgeably with lawyers and provides a useful tool to share with lawyers • Assists them in reinterpreting their work from a human rights perspective • Makes it easy to identify which conventions and which paragraphs within conventions would be of greatest interest in their work or to advocate around a certain position.	1 & 2. Useful contacts with organizations and/or lawyers working on the issue • Different expertise (e.g. desktop publishing or other skills your group may lack) • Ideas on how the manual should be developed and used • Research assistance or other input to reduce your group's workload • Resources to add to the resource list (e.g. names and addresses of other groups, relevant periodicals) • They may want to do a community action manual on another issue that is of particular importance to them and can later be combined with yours to make a more comprehensive country document.
2. Community Groups	2. As above, plus: Easy to access for those not necessarily interested in women's issues • Useful for them to know what the debate is on certain issues since these debates may surface in their own discussions.	see above.
3. Women's Affairs Depts. at all levels (focal points, ministers, etc.)	3. Ready reference guide • A timesaver that provides a short, easy to read overview with key points • Gives information on which ministries and groups are working on an issue • Can be used to argue points with other government officials; to inform work with counterparts in other countries; and to give weight and validity to efforts for change on behalf of women • Can be used when speaking to groups as part of education effort.	3. Information on which government ministries are reponsible for reporting • Information on national laws and where government stands in relation to reform.
4. Lawyers	4. Useful to have extracted aspects of conventions (since many lawyers have not worked on international law since college) • Identifies exact paragraph relating to issue for ease of location in total convention when working with original • Provides information on where to get total text • Useful to know cases where convention has been used to change national laws • Offers contacts with lawyers elsewhere working on international law in this way • Lists groups working on the issue.	4. Knowledge of national laws means s/he can match these with the Conventions • Likely to have access to Internet so could download Conventions.

Handout 2
"Information Finder"

1. **For the full text of the UN conventions cited in this manual:** You will find Web site addresses for several UN agencies, also the following institutions, all of which have convention text online: University of Minnesota (USA) Human Rights Library; the International Centre for Human Rights and Democratic Development; and Internet Resources for Women's Legal and Public Policy Information. See pp. 120-121

   If you do not have access to the Internet, you will find other places listed on pp. 15-16. Also, check the UN Information Centres—there are 70 worldwide—and university holdings in your country.

2. **For the basic human rights documents:** Women and Human Rights: The Basic Documents, is a compilation of the full text of the principal international agreements that are referred to in this manual. It is available for US$18 (plus postage) from Women, Ink. Ordering information on pp. 146-148.

3. **The reporting procedure for the convention you are working with, and how to contact the relevant convention committee:** Each convention establishes the enforcement and complaint procedures to be used in monitoring government compliance with it. For a brief overview of these different enforcement mechanisms, see pp. 9-15. There is a chart listing those conventions which have established committees of experts who are responsible on p. 10.

4. **For human rights mechanisms:** There is an excellent and detailed description of how to use these in *Women's Human Rights Step by Step: A Practical Guide to Using International Human Rights Law and Mechanisms to Defend Women's Human Rights*. It is available through Women, Ink. for US$27.00. Ordering information on pp. 146-148.

5. **For your country's report to the relevant convention committee:** In general, your government's Ministry of Foreign Affairs is responsible for submitting your country's report to the respective committee. As your country's report is considered a public document, you can also request one from the United Nations. See UN addresses on p.15.

6. **For when your country is scheduled to report to a treaty committee:** Contact the UN High Commission for Human Rights (UNHCHR) and request the reporting schedule specific to your country. You will find the address for UNHCHR on p. 15.

7. **For what reservations your country has made to a particular convention:** Check the UN Web site <http://www.un.org> and look under "Treaties." If you do not have access to the Internet, call the Attorney General's office in your country.

8. **For whether your country has signed or ratified a particular convention:** Ratification charts, organized by region and country for all the conventions referred to in this manual, are on pp. 127-135.

9. **For the related laws of your country:** You will need to work with lawyers in your country to determine which laws have been changed and which still need to be changed in order to comply with the terms of the convention.

10. **For the ministry responsible for implementation in your country:** Start with the ministry responsible for foreign affairs in your country. They will direct you to another department if necessary.

11. **For more reading resources on the topic:** Check the Using Information Technology section for organizations with collections (pp. 103-124). Another excellent source of women's human rights information is Women, Ink. which makes available for purchase human rights publications from organizations world wide. You will find a current Women, Ink. resource listing on p. 147.

A Tribunal:

FACT

At community and country levels worldwide, women are organizing tribunals with anywhere from a few dozen to a thousand or more participants. They have found tribunals to be compelling fora for documenting and making visible violations against women's human rights.

In June 1993, at the NGO Forum held during the United Nations World Conference on Human Rights in Vienna, a 68-year-old woman from a rural village in Korea stood before an audience of a thousand people to give testimony. The women and men seated before her, hailing from more than a hundred countries, included community leaders, human rights activists, UN delegates and other high-ranking government officials. Also present were a panel of human rights experts, there to listen and respond to the 32 women testifiers, who, like the Korean woman before them, had come to tell their stories of gross violations against their human rights.

Clothed in full-length traditional dress, the Korean woman stepped up to the microphone and began to speak. "I was only 14 when the Japanese soldiers came to my village," she said. "They forced all the girls into trucks and drove us away, saying they needed waitresses." Instead, these young women were taken to military camps to begin a life of unspeakable cruelty and humiliation. "I had never been with a man and knew nothing about sex," she continued. "Terrified, I was forced to lie on my back on a filthy wooden floor. The tiny cell was hardly the width and length of my body. Then the soldiers began arriving. They forced themselves onto me, one after another, day after day, night after night. Some days there were more than 40, with no rest in between. My body became so ripped and torn that I frequently had to be stitched back together. When the wounds healed a little, I would be returned to the room for the raping to continue. I became numb to life and gave up all hope of ever seeing my country or my family again."

The room was hushed. The woman's quiet voice never wavered. But when she told of arriving home and, after a time, finally telling her mother what had happened, her voice suddenly cracked and tears began to fall down her cheeks. Someone stepped forward and asked if she wanted the cameras and floodlights turned off. "No!" she responded firmly. "I've waited 50 years to tell my story and the world must know so another woman's life is not destroyed like mine!"

For those in the audience, the woman's testimony provoked a mixture of outrage and admiration. The details of the story were painful to hear but her courage in telling it so many years later touched people deeply. Her testimony, along with those of the 32 other women, was at the heart of a well-planned campaign undertaken by women's human rights activists from around the world. The campaign drew on the expertise of women's groups from every world region. There were lawyers who advised on legal terminology, political strategists who contributed their expertise in engaging government delegates, women's human rights activists who added

Making Women's Voices Heard

their experience and that of their organizations and journalists who advised on ways to capture media attention. Together they created an event that triggered not only worldwide attention to violations of women's rights, but also significant changes in international human rights policy statements. Achievements included:

- major coverage by most global media—TV, radio and print—effectively casting a worldwide spotlight on violations of women's human rights;

- sensitization to the issues surrounding women's human rights amongst key decision-makers from 171 Member States of the United Nations participating in the World Conference on Human Rights;

- recognition within the Vienna Programme of Action that violence against women is a violation of human rights;

- adoption of a UN Declaration on Violence Against Women;

- inclusion of an entire section on women's human rights within the Vienna Declaration (a separate document to the Vienna Programme of Action), and a statement that proclaimed, "the human rights of women and the girl-child are an indivisible part of universal human rights;" and

- appointment of a UN Special Rapporteur on Violence Against Women.

Beyond media coverage and conference achievements, however, the Vienna Global Tribunal on Violations of Women's Human Rights, and the activities worldwide that preceded it, brought about a new sense of empowerment on the part of the global women's movement.

Above all, it gave birth to a new activist strategy of hearings and tribunals that was taken back home by NGO and government delegates, bringing women's human rights violations to the forefront in towns and communities worldwide.

> *Will there be a case against Mirko Lukic, a Kljuc Chetnik whose entire army company raped Mrs. Omeragic in her own home, and who also rammed a rifle barrel into her womb?*

— Fadila Memisevic, Zenic Centre for the Registration of War and Genocide Crimes, Bosnia/Herzegovina.

HOLDING A TRIBUNAL

Tribunals in Action: Bringing it Home

> *In 1987, I was a victim of a murder attempt by my former boyfriend, who...set my body on fire in front of my four-year-old son, saying that if I would not die I would look so physically disfigured that nobody would recognize me and no man would want me.... (T)he police have not registered the crime.*
>
> —Maria Celsa da Conceiçao, Brazil

At community and country levels worldwide, women are organizing tribunals with anywhere from a few dozen to a thousand or more participants. They have found tribunals to be both compelling fora for documenting and making visible violations against women's human rights as well as effective mechanisms for challenging governments to protect those rights. While tribunals are not legal proceedings per se and the "judges," or panels of experts, do not have the power to enforce recommendations, tribunals nonetheless have affected significant changes in attitudes and policies concerning women. Here are some examples.

In Africa, the YWCA of Zambia organized a tribunal in which battered women testified about the violence they suffered at the hands of family members. At the end of the tribunal, the panel of experts recommended stricter sentences for perpetrators as well as the acceptance of "cumulative provocation" as a defence in cases where women kill their abusive husbands. The incorporation of the Convention on the Elimination of All Forms of Discrimination Against Women (CEDAW) into the country's national laws was also advocated.

Also in Africa, the Tanzania Media Women's Association (TAMWA) staged a tribunal at the same time as a criminal case was being tried in court involving an 18-year-old woman who was drugged, abducted and sexually abused. The goal of the tribunal was to encourage community members to make appearances in court; their presence alone, it was believed, would result in a conviction and a stiffer sentence for the defendant. The tribunal worked: The defendant was sentenced to 17 years in prison and ordered to pay damages to the woman. With the momentum from the tribunal, the community established its own human right's centre.

In Asia, the Asian Women's Human Rights Council (AWHRC) and the Women's Human Rights Committee of Japan (WHRCJ) organized a tribunal on sex trafficking and war crimes committed against women. Seventeen women from 11 Asian countries spoke eloquently about their torture and enslavement. Following the testimonies, a distinguished group of judges gave their recommendations and helped form an eight-point plan of action.

Tribunals have also explored other themes—e.g. violations of women's economic rights—and employed a variety of experimental tactics. In one case the participants at a tribunal became the enforcers of the judges' recommendations!

In other words, unlike other types of official proceedings, tribunals are flexible. There is no single "right" way to hold them.

HOLDING A TRIBUNAL

Five Steps for Organizing a Tribunal

Step 1
■ **Define Themes, Objectives and Outcomes...**

Decide which human rights issues are in most need of public support and attention. You may want to address more than one issue. Single-theme hearings are inclined to be more highly focused.

Step 2
■ **Plan the Basics...**

Consider who will be testifying and who will be listening. Factor in sufficient time for moderators to speak and judges to present opening and closing remarks. Decide on a convenient location. Create a programme guide for participants, maybe a poster.

Step 3
■ **Develop a Media Strategy...**

A tribunal is usually considered very "newsworthy" by the print, radio, TV and electronic press. Therefore, develop a strategy that will leverage this power.

Step 4
■ **Map Out a Tribunal Process...**

By insisting on an inclusive and democratic process—one that is sensitive to women's needs—tribunals provide us with a new image of justice.

Step 5
■ **Plan the Follow-up...**

Follow-up is critical to tribunals, from both a logistical and moral point of view. Testifiers need support in the period after the tribunal occurs and before any legislative or policy action takes place; they require protection against reprisals and will benefit greatly from a sense of solidarity if their situation changes in any way.

HOLDING A TRIBUNAL

Step 1 DEFINE THEMES, OBJECTIVES AND OUTCOMES

"I think we should focus on violence against women at our first tribunal."

The first step in organizing a tribunal is deciding which human rights issues are most in need of public support and attention. You may want to address more than one issue in your tribunal; interconnecting themes often generate additional interest, a wider audience and greater momentum. Single-theme hearings are inclined to be more highly focused. It may be helpful to organize a tribunal around an issue that is actively being investigated or discussed by local or regional groups because the tribunal can bring increased visibility to the discussion.

After deciding which issues you wish to focus on, it's time to clearly define the objectives and potential outcomes of your tribunal. While tribunals are not official legal proceedings, they can meet specific objectives and achieve concrete outcomes. By planning strategically, and realistically, you are more likely to streamline your planning activities, meet your objectives, achieve the desired outcomes and present a strong and clear message to the press about the tribunal. A tribunal can have many objectives, such as:

...to promote awareness, understanding and empowerment

- to achieve recognition of certain issues as women's human rights issues,

- to document, define and make visible violations of women's human rights,

- to challenge some of the existing thoughts and images people have of women and violence against women,

- to sensitize attendees, including government officials and those in power, to women's human rights issues,

HOLDING A TRIBUNAL

- to publicize the high occurrence of crimes against women across cultures and nationalities,

- to illustrate how the law, social policy, cultural norms, economics and media contribute to the perpetuation of the subordinate status and exploitative and oppressive conditions of women,

- to empower women who testify as well as those who listen.

...to influence action and enforcement

- to galvanize organizers and attendees around a human rights issue,

- to influence funders as they make support decisions,

- to make accountable those who continue to violate women's human rights,

- to evaluate the effectiveness of existing human rights policies and procedures,

- to put political and moral pressure on policy makers at the local, national and international levels to promote women's human rights,

- to influence negotiations that may be in process around a human rights issue,

- to challenge and change existing laws and urge enactment of laws that advance women's rights,

- to create new mechanisms for preventing, tracking and redressing violations against women's human rights,

- to define other concrete actions that governments, organizations and women may take around a human rights issues.

> *I come to give a testimony about the difficulties, persecutions and situations that affect our lives as lesbian women. I am going to talk in order to make visible the situation that affects many absent sisters and many who are present here today.*
>
> — Rebeca Sevilla, Peru.

"Now that we've decided on the themes and objectives for the tribunal, we need to select testifiers, judges and support persons."

TAKING ACTION **97**

HOLDING A TRIBUNAL

Step 2 — PLAN THE BASICS

"I know several women who could testify about gross violations of their rights."

Once you have established your purpose, discuss the practicalities:

■ Pinpoint Key Players…

Testifiers

Testifiers should be selected according to two main criteria: a woman's need to testify (i.e. the seriousness of the violation she has suffered) and her effectiveness (i.e. her ability to recount her story in a manner that will reach many people). In some cases, due to the threat of repercussions, financial constraints, language barriers etc., a representative should be chosen to deliver someone's firsthand account. Such advocates may include delegates from human rights NGOs, women who are active regionally, and people working in government or UN agencies.

Support Persons

Because testifying can be traumatic, morale building is a critical element in preparing testifiers. Consider assigning each testifier a support person who will accompany her throughout the proceedings. This person could double as a translator for the testifier as well.

Judges

Judges need not be practicing adjudicators or experts in women's human rights. What matters most is that they are people who are supportive of women's rights issues, influential among policy makers and shapers of public opinion or able to attract media attention.

Other Important Roles

These might include a logistics person, a liaison person who can work with other regional, national and international groups, a media person, a chronicler and a follow-up person.

■ Design the Programme…

To design the tribunal programme, consider who will be testifying and listening. Each presentation should be concise and to the point; 10 minutes is generally an adequate block of time for testifiers. Factor in sufficient time for moderators to speak and judges to present opening and closing remarks. Sequence your sessions so there's a natural flow to your overall program, building in time for meals, coffee breaks

HOLDING A TRIBUNAL

and perhaps travel time from one building or room to another. No matter how urgent the issue you choose to address is, people need time-out for physical as well as emotional refreshment. Also set aside enough time during the planning stage for moderators to prepare testifiers as well as for an orientation session where participants can meet and review their testimonies.

Depending on your theme, you may be able to enhance your programme if you hold the tribunal on a day that will be getting attention on its own merits (such as International Women's Day, March 8; International Day to End Violence, November 25; International Human Rights Day, December 10). Take into account your constituency's schedules. If you convene your hearing on a Wednesday afternoon, will participants be able to afford to take a day off work? If you hold the tribunal on the weekend, will there be sufficient media coverage?

■ Think about Logistics...

A location that is easily accessible by foot, car or public transportation is crucial. In addition, if you want to hold your tribunal concurrently with another conference, consider whether convening in close proximity to that event will be a benefit or a drawback to your tribunal. Consider the size of the meeting space and the equipment you will need (microphones, slide projectors, video screens, translation systems etc.). Investigate whether your space is wheelchair accessible.

■ Create Tribunal Materials...

You may also want to consider producing a programme guide for participants, audio/videotapes for use as teaching materials, and perhaps some posters, which can be a useful reminder of the event and can be used in classrooms as well as offices. T-shirts are great as fund-raisers and as identifying garb for the organizers.

HOLDING A TRIBUNAL

Step 3 — DEVELOP A MEDIA STRATEGY

A tribunal is usually considered very "newsworthy" by the print, radio, TV and electronic press. Therefore, develop a strategy that will leverage this power.

- **Create a Publicity Plan...**
You can announce hearings through radio, TV, newspapers and the Internet. Send faxes and e-mail to any organization that may help get the word out.

- **Develop a Press Release...**
and/or press kit—a must if you want to work with the press. Since many journalists are not familiar with women's human rights, materials included in the kit should give as much background information as possible. Include short biographies of the testifiers and judges, names of organizations and NGOs that work on human rights, a glossary of terms and a bibliography of human rights resources.

- **Select Human Rights Internet Sites...**
that are going to be most useful to you in giving visibility to the event.

- **Create a "Press Room"...**
to enhance the coverage of the event by the media as well as allow you some input into the slant the media takes. A well-equipped press room can offer a quiet place for interviews, provide informative fliers, books, videotapes, articles and fact sheets and serve as a general resource centre.

- **Develop and Distribute Post-Tribunal Materials ...**
Organizers of the 1993 Vienna Global Tribunal arranged for a print transcript and video of the proceedings. These are excellent resource materials, and are now being used by journalists, schools and community groups worldwide.

A word of caution: Media attention can sometimes backfire. While coverage can be advantageous, mainstream media may sensationalize your tribunal, report it with an unfortunate sexist bias and depict testifiers as yet another group of women victims. This is not helpful in promoting women's human rights. If this does happen, it may indicate the need for follow-up action to sensitize the press and the community, perhaps by offering training to better understand the issues.

HOLDING A TRIBUNAL

Step 4: MAP OUT A TRIBUNAL PROCESS

Tribunals are very different from typical judicial proceedings, which are often inaccessible, threatening or demeaning to women. By insisting on an inclusive and democratic process—one that is sensitive to women's needs—tribunals provide us with a new image of justice. Indeed, this is one of the keys to an effective tribunal. The other key to an effective tribunal is establishing credibility with the attendees and the press. Here are some suggestions for accomplishing both:

- **Establish fair and concrete criteria** for selecting testifiers and share them with everyone involved in the process.

- **Decide on the nature and scope of the testimonies.** Will the testifiers describe, identify or clarify specific examples of human rights violations? Will they report on human rights investigations? Will they identify the laws or standards or obligations that have been broken? Will they outline their demands for redress?

- **Allow equal access, treatment and time** to those who are implicated by the testifiers. Give them ample and fair notice of the implications as well as the opportunity to refute them.

- **Pay attention to any conflicts of interest** that may surface with testifiers, judges, or other participants.

- **Select judges who have demonstrated their integrity** and who are respected in the community.

- **Assure that testimony is accurate,** well-documented and not based on hearsay.

- **Discourage testifiers from being melodramatic**; the stories are powerful enough.

- **Select a "friend of the tribunal,"** someone who can function as an impartial master of ceremonies, offer syntheses of the testimonies and recommendations and keep the tribunal on track. A fair and active "friend" can ensure that the tribunal runs smoothly, which will add to an overall positive image.

- **Allow for the presentation of supplementary materials** such as UN documents or NGO statements that can add important perspectives to the human rights issues.

TAKING ACTION 101

HOLDING A TRIBUNAL

Step 5 PLAN THE FOLLOW-UP

BOOKS

SELECTED PUBLICATIONS FROM WOMEN, INK.*

Demanding Accountability: The Global Campaign and Vienna Tribunal for Women's Human Rights
Charlotte Bunch and Niamh Reilly
A comprehensive history and analysis of women's organizing around the UN World Conference on Human Rights, with detailed insights into the Tribunal.
Center for Women's Global Leadership/UNIFEM, 1994. $15.00

The Right to Live Without Violence: Women's Proposals and Actions
Reports on the Tribunal on Violations of Women's Human Rights in El Salvador (1993) and examines legal provisions on violence in the region.
Latin American and Caribbean Women's Health Network, 1996. $25.00

Without Reservation: The Beijing Tribunal on Accountability for Women's Human Rights
Niamh Reilly (Ed.)
Documents the last in the series of tribunals held at major UN conferences.
Center for Women's Global Leadership, 1996. $15.00

* Contact information on page 146.

"It was such an incredible tribunal, I must get the word out to the press right away."

Follow-up is critical to tribunals, not only from a logistical point of view but from a moral point of view. Testifiers need support in the period after the tribunal occurs and before any legislative or policy action takes place; they require protection against reprisals and they will benefit from a sense of solidarity if their situation changes in any way.

There is also a responsibility to other human rights activists who may benefit from your tribunal and to the various UN bodies and officials who focus on human rights. They can press for resolutions and sanctions against state violators of human rights, but only if they have credible evidence of these violations. (For more information on how to report violations to the UN, see Section 1.)

The type of follow-up you do depends on the purpose for which you're holding the tribunal. If, for example, it is used as an awareness-raising vehicle, you might set up ongoing meetings with attending journalists to help expand their coverage of women's rights issues. If your tribunal is being held to address legislative concerns, your follow-up might focus on monitoring developments in the legal field.

Some general suggestions for follow-up activities include:

- **Assign a follow-up person...**
  to maintain contact with testifiers and to serve as a liaison between the women and your group.

- **Publicize the outcome...**
  of the tribunal in newsletters or reports on the Internet.

- **Send copies of transcripts...**
  to local legislators and policy makers.

- **Pressure policy makers...**
  to act upon those issues raised during the tribunal.

- **Highlight any changes in behaviour, policy or laws...**
  that occurred because of the tribunal.

- **Contact journalists with new information on tribunal results.**

Information Tools: Building Human Rights Communities

On 7 July, 1996, Fatou Dieng fled her house having suffered violent blows from her husband Ousmane Sall, a retired Senegalese army colonel. According to reports from the medical facility that treated her, Fatou had bruises and contusions all over her body and one eye and ear were so badly damaged she risked losing them. This was not the first time Fatou had been beaten. But it was the first time in 22 years of domestic violence that she decided to complain. She filed a complaint for intentional grievous bodily harm and asked for a divorce.

Prosecuting a husband, much less a high-ranking officer, is never easy. But within days, word of Fatou's case traveled through the Internet and women activists all over the globe responded, writing letters, sending faxes and reminding Senegalese leaders that their country had ratified most of the international agreements protecting women's human rights. Thanks to this instant international pressure, Colonel Ousmane Sall was put in jail and fined one million francs.

Fatou's case continues in the courts and has been taken up by the Centre Against Violence Against Women. It is just one example of how electronic communications can help women mobilize for human rights. Computers and electronic communications are information tools that are fast becoming an integral part of local and global strategies to demand, protect and defend women's human rights. Activists and advocates are finding that these tools—including e-mail, the Internet, the World Wide Web and electronic lists and conferences—can help bring attention to human rights violations, mobilize action, and demand accountability in ways not possible before. When used in conjunction with other communication devices, such as telephones, faxes and letters, they can help create a women's human rights community that is millions strong.

HOW HUMAN RIGHTS

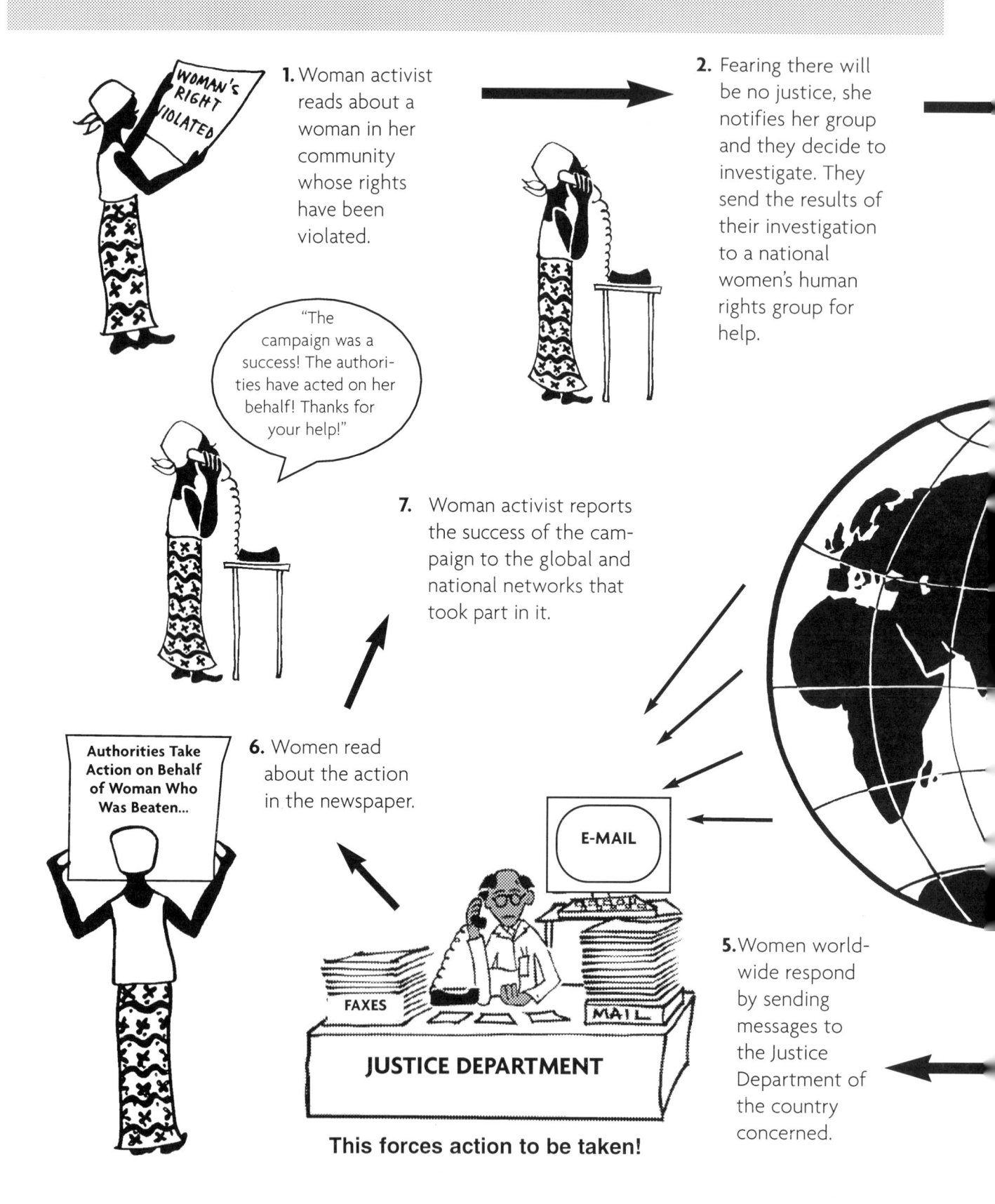

1. Woman activist reads about a woman in her community whose rights have been violated.

2. Fearing there will be no justice, she notifies her group and they decide to investigate. They send the results of their investigation to a national women's human rights group for help.

"The campaign was a success! The authorities have acted on her behalf! Thanks for your help!"

7. Woman activist reports the success of the campaign to the global and national networks that took part in it.

6. Women read about the action in the newspaper.

Authorities Take Action on Behalf of Woman Who Was Beaten...

E-MAIL

FAXES

MAIL

JUSTICE DEPARTMENT

5. Women worldwide respond by sending messages to the Justice Department of the country concerned.

This forces action to be taken!

104 RIGHTS OF WOMEN

NEWS TRAVELS

3. The national group, on receiving the information, calls a meeting of other groups, and they all decide to launch a global campaign by sending an action alert via e-mail, fax and mail. The action alert calls upon women to write to the proper authorities to protest the violation of the woman's rights.

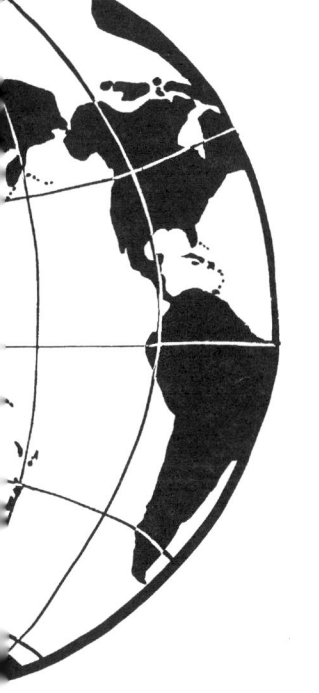

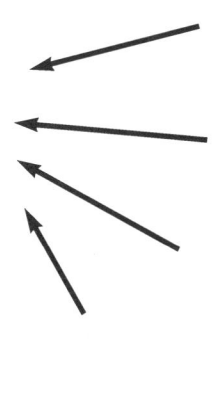

FAX MACHINE

MAIL BOX

E-MAIL

COMPUTER

MODEM

PHONE LINE

4. Networks pick up the campaign, sending the action alert to their groups via e-mail, fax and mail.

TAKING ACTION **105**

USING INFORMATION TOOLS

Seeing how new technologies can be revolutionary . . .

A woman in Senegal is beaten and within weeks more than ten million women know about her suffering. All over the globe, people concerned with women's human rights are using electronic technologies to broadcast violations and prompt action. Women worldwide are using these tools in many ways:

- An e-mail and fax appeal sent from Chad resulted in a stream of letters and faxes that helped protect a Chadian journalist from the effects of a *fatwa* that had been issued against her because of a video she had made on female genital mutilation.

- In the United States, one town put the names of domestic violence offenders onto its World Wide Web site to make them publicly known and to deter other potential offenders.

- People concerned with ending violence against women may participate in a global electronic conference that serves as a place to share strategies and experiences.

- And no matter where we live, if we can access the Internet via a modem attached to both a computer and a phone line, we can get a copy of the key human rights conventions, or follow the meetings of the Committee on the Elimination of All Forms of Discrimination Against Women (CEDAW) from home or school.

Through the Internet, we can connect with women who may live thousands of miles away but who face similar dangers and challenges. We can find distant allies and fellow activists willing to take action on our behalf. In this way, new technologies are helping to build a global human rights community—one that is not defined by geographical boundaries or national frontiers. Instead, we can magnify and multiply our voices with women all over the world so that our concerns are heard.

USING INFORMATION TOOLS

...or exclusionary

For most of us, seeing how electronic communications or computers are supporting human rights work is the easy part. The difficulty comes with a decision to move forward: What happens to those of us who cannot afford computers or e-mail, who live in countries without Internet access or whose governments strictly limit, control or monitor electronic communications? What about those of us for whom e-mail is very costly to send and receive? Or those of us who need training but have no one qualified to teach us? Or those who don't read the predominant languages found on the Internet? Will we be excluded from these new communities?

Equipment, access and training—these are just some of the challenges posed by new technologies. There's also the issue of accuracy (can information on the Internet be trusted?) and a legitimate concern that information can be, and often is, misused. Information overload—too much information—is another problem for many human rights activists.

These are all complex issues that require thought and action; they are not, however, within the scope of this workbook. (For an excellent resource on these issues, see the forthcoming *Women@Internet: Creating New Cultures in Cyberspace*, edited by Wendy Harcourt, Zed Books, London, December 1998. Soon to be available through Women, Ink.)

Instead, we offer a series of starting points for making use of computers and electronic networking, and for combining these tools with other non-electronic strategies so as to be as inclusive as possible. We do so in the belief that making use of new information technologies is critical for women's human rights activists and that finding strategies to help address global imbalances in infrastructure and access is equally important.

"I'm ready to start with the Internet. Where shall I begin?"

TAKING ACTION 107

USING INFORMATION TOOLS

Three ideas for using new information technologies

FACT

Electronic mailing lists and conferences enable human rights activists to share information in different ways.

1 SHARE INFORMATION
Mobilize for action via electronic mailing lists, conferences, networks and Web sites.

2 RECORD INFORMATION
Document human rights violations with help from computer networks, databases and formats.

3 PRODUCE INFORMATION
Become an information provider through desktop and Web publishing. In this way, you can produce information that can be accessed by the millions of people that have access to e-mail and/or Internet.

Equipment and services required

1. COMPUTER
You need one with a at least 16 megs of RAM, i.e. Random Access Memory, or processing memory.

2. MODEM
This connects your computer to your phone line. It either comes already installed (with newer computers) or needs to be purchased separately and plugged into your computer.

3. PHONE LINE
You access the Internet via your phone line. The modem is plugged into this line.

4. NETWORK SERVICE PROVIDER
This service connects you to the Internet via a phone call. Find the cheapest, most efficient network service provider at your library or from someone already on the Internet.

USING INFORMATION TOOLS

SHARE INFORMATION 1

"I just found out how to use e-mail. Now we can do a letter-writing campaign."

Sharing information is very important to the growth of a well-informed women's human rights community. Whether it is to organize a global letter-writing campaign in support of an action or to report a human rights violation within your own community, new information technologies—particularly electronic mailing lists and conferences—offer activists speed and extended outreach.

If you want to send out an action alert to many individuals and groups all at the same time then an electronic mailing list is probably your best method. An electronic mailing list allows you to reach many people by sending a message to a single address. It is often referred to as a "listserv" or "majordomo." Anyone who can send and receive e-mail can be a part of a listserv. The message is sent out once and it is automatically copied to everyone on the list. This method is also excellent for ongoing discussions of human rights issues and for creating two-way communication channels or "spaces" where people interested in a common topic can e-mail messages to one another on a regular basis.

Another way to get ideas from other human rights activists and share thoughts around a specific subject or issue is by visiting an electronic conference or forum where all the messages from participants are gathered in one place. Some electronic conferences are "members-only," or available only to the customers of a particular Internet provider (for example, only members of the Association for Progressive Communications [APC] network—an international Internet provider for not-for-profit groups and activities—can access APC fora). Other electronic conferences are available on the Web to anyone with Web access.

Unlike mailing lists, electronic conferences are hosted in one central location. When you visit, you see a "menu" of topics containing all the comments people have posted to the forum so far. You can search through the topics, read messages and post a reply directly to the conference. It's also possible to "connect" members-only conferences to mailing lists, so that some members follow it on the conference and others follow it on the mailing list (ask your network service provider for instructions).

Web-based fora are open to all people with Web access and so reach a different and wider audience than member-only fora. Although less private and select than either member-only conferences or mailing lists, they are quite easy to use and will undoubtedly become more popular as access to the Web improves around the world.

Reduce information overload. Send a summary of any long document first and offer to e-mail the full document only to those who want it. Or produce an electronic "digest" or summary of the discussions in a mailing list and offer it as an alternative to receiving every message on the list.

TAKING ACTION 109

USING INFORMATION TOOLS

The Many Ways to Use Electronic Mailing Lists and Conferences

Human Rights activists use electronic mailing lists and conferences to share information in different ways.

Be an information multiplier. Print and pass on human rights information you find online. Give it to your library, put it in a newsletter or fax it!

ONE TO MANY

One group or person shares information with many others. This is usually done with a list, not through a conference, and only requires that you have access to e-mail. Example: the International Women's Tribune Centre (IWTC) publishes a biweekly bulletin called IWTC Women's GlobalNet that shares information received from groups and individuals worldwide about activities, initiatives and events undertaken by, for and about women. IWTC sends the bulletin to a list of approx. 750 (English-language) and 400 (Spanish-language) e-mail "multiplier" addresses, and another 500 fax "multiplier" numbers. Each "multiplier" group then e-mails or faxes the bulletin on to their networks, reaching tens of thousands of groups and individuals. To become part of this list, send an e-mail to ‹iwtc@igc.apc.org› or fax (1-212) 661-2704. Mention that you want to be part of the IWTC Women's GlobalNet.

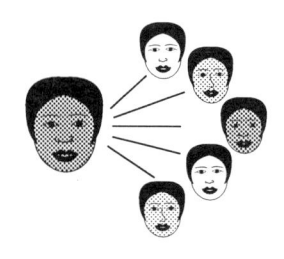

FEW TO FEW

Lists or conferences are especially useful when activities need to be coordinated and/or shared between members in a specific network. A good example of this is the conference set up by Women Living Under Muslim Laws (WLUML). It is composed of 30 regional and national coordination groups, out of which 18 have access to e-mail. It further distributes international alerts for action electronically to 120 people. For more information on this, send an e-mail to WLUML at ‹wluml@mnet.fr›.

MANY TO MANY

Both electronic lists and conferences facilitate communication among many groups and individuals, particularly those with common issues and concerns. One example of such a group is Feminists Against Violence Network (FAVNET). Members of this group include: human rights activists, legal advocates, torture survivors and concerned citizens who seek to redress violence against women. For more information, send an e-mail to ‹favnet@otd.com›.

110 RIGHTS OF WOMEN

USING INFORMATION TOOLS

Women are creating a women's human rights community that is millions strong.

> The task of human rights organizations is to put these 'pictures of truth' into one cohesive report which is as objective as possible, reflecting the actual events. The formats must allow for the recording of information from particular sources as well as for the recording and communicating of the composite picture created by the human rights organization on behalf of the victim.

— HURIDOCS Standard Formats: A Tool for Documenting Human Rights Violations.

> (Where) governments count on ignorance and silence, information and communication are our best weapons.

Patty Whaley
Amnesty International

> The difficulty for us in using electronic solidarity alerts is that many women's groups in Francophone Africa [do not have access] to computers. We have to combine different ways of communication for alerts— from personal contacts to telephone, fax and e-mail where available.

Activist in Senegal

> Using e-mail, we've been able to catch an incoming story in the morning, issue an urgent action by midday and pick up the media report on our urgent action before we go home for dinner. That speed can be just the edge we need to save a life.

Amnesty International activist.

TAKING ACTION

USING INFORMATION TOOLS

Searching for human rights electronic mailing lists or electronic conferences

A search engine can help you find the e-mail addresses of people, businesses or organizations on the Internet.

Alta Vista is one that allows you to search in any of 24 different languages. You can visit it at ‹www.altavista.digital.com›.

Before your group sets out to find, and/or create, a list or conference that would be most appropriate to your needs, think about what type of organizing activity you would like to pursue. Is it a one-time campaign that you want to launch? Is your group involved in an ongoing human rights discussion?

Once you've defined your purpose, find out which human rights mailing lists and conferences already exist; there might be lists and conferences already set up that are appropriate for your group's activities which you could join. When you join a list or conference, you might consider becoming an information focal point for your community. In this way, you could take information from the list or conference and share it through newsletters, bulletins or faxes with those who don't have computers.

Here are the addresses of human rights mailing lists as well as places to search for other lists. Some may require that you subscribe to the list, and you need to check out how to do that with the contact address given.

CURRENT HUMAN RIGHTS LISTS

THE WOMEN'S NETWORKING SUPPORT PROGRAMME OF THE ASSOCIATION FOR PROGRESSIVE COMMUNICATIONS (APC) helps women's rights activists and NGOs use computer communications in their work. The programme provides technical training, a directory of network contacts and e-mail and Web services.
Web site: ‹http://www.apc.org/apcwomen›.
You can find a list of other APC networks in your area at:
E-mail: ‹apc-brochure@igc.apc.org›
Web site:
‹http://www.apc.org/members.html›

AMNESTY INTERNATIONAL (AI)
This list is composed of activists worldwide fighting against human rights violations. AI sends out a regular bulletin of news releases from its international secretariat in London, England. To subscribe, send the message noted below to the following e-mail address:
E-mail: ‹majordomo@oil.ca›
Message: subscribe amnesty-L

FEMINISTS AGAINST VIOLENCE NETWORK (FAVNET)
This list is composed of groups and individuals dedicated to ending domestic violence and violence against women through networking and direct action in a feminist environment. To subscribe, send the message noted below to the following e-mail address:
E-mail: ‹majordomo@otd.com›
Message: subscribe favnet ‹then place your e-mail address here›

USING INFORMATION TOOLS

HUMAN RIGHTS INFORMATION AND DOCUMENTATION SYSTEMS INTERNATIONAL (HURIDOCS)

HURIDOCS is one of the oldest and most comprehensive lists available. Members of this network receive regular bulletins including articles, reports and announcements on the handling of human rights information. To subscribe, send the message noted below to the following e-mail address:
E-mail: ‹majordomo@mail.comlink.apc.org›
Message: subscribe huridocs-gen-l

HUMAN RIGHTS INFORMATION NETWORK-WOMEN (HURINET-WOMEN)

HURINet is a human rights information service comprised of multilingual information on all aspects of human rights on an international level. HURINet distributes bulletins, reports, urgent actions, appeals for help, petitions and organizational information to a wide variety of recipients around the world. HURINet-Women focuses specifically on international human rights concerning women.
Contact: Debra Guzman
E-mail: ‹debra@oln.comlink.apc.org›

NETWORK OF EAST-WEST WOMEN (NEWW)

This network focuses on women's legal rights issues, especially in the post-communist countries of Eastern and Central Europe. To subscribe in English, send the message noted below to the following e-mail address:
E-mail: ‹majordomo@igc.apc.org›
Message: subscribe neww-rights
To subscribe in Russian, send a message to the following e-mail address:
E-mail: ‹neww@glas.apc.org›.
Contact: Irina Doskich or Galina Venediktova

BEIJING-CONF

This list is supported by the United Nations Development Programme. It includes discussions on issues that arose from the 1995 Beijing Conference and focuses on implementing the Platform for Action. To subscribe, send the message noted below to the following e-mail address:
E-mail: ‹majordomo@confer.edc.org›
Message: subscribe Beijing-conf

BEIJING 95-L

This is a forum for discussions on the United Nations Fourth World Conference on Women, Beijing, China, in September 1995. Topics include post-conference events and reports. To subscribe, send the message noted below to the following e-mail address:
E-mail: ‹listserv@netcom.com›
Message: subscribe Beijing 95-L ‹your name› ‹your e-mail address›

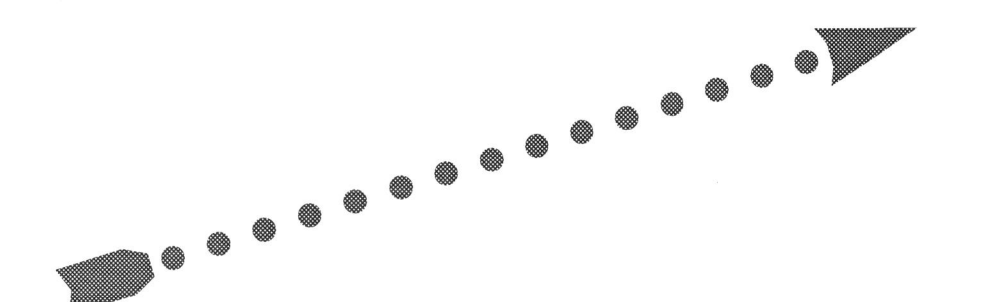

When responding to e-mails, do not automatically include the original copy of the letter (referred to as "quoting"). This can add more pages to the response, and waste time and money for many groups.

RESOURCE

Getting Online for Human Rights: Some Frequently Asked Questions and Answers about Using the Internet in Human Rights Work
This manual is forthcoming from: AAAS Science and Human Rights Program, 1200 New York Avenue NW, Washington, DC 20005, **USA**
e-mail: ‹shrp@aaas.org›

TAKING ACTION 113

USING INFORMATION TOOLS

Searching for human rights lists ... globally

Add a fax broadcast service (sending a fax to a large list of fax numbers) to reach people without e-mail. Some businesses offer fax broadcast services that send faxes late at night when rates are low. Lists of fax numbers can also be programmed into your fax machine, or into your computer!

LISZT

This is a mailing list directory that enables you to search by topic or issue area. To reach this address however, you need access to the World Wide Web, which not everyone has. World Wide Web addresses always begin with <http://www.>. The address for Liszt is: <http://www.liszt.com/>.

The following names and addresses from various regions of the world are contacts who can help you locate lists and conferences in your specific region or area of interest.

... in Francophone Africa

Contact Marie Helene Mottin-Sylla, Environment and Development Action in the Third World (ENDA) and Synergy Gender and Development (SYNFEV), Dakar, Senegal.
E-mail: <mhms@enda.sn>

... in Eastern Africa

Contact Mercy Wambui, Kenya.
E-mail: <mwambui@iconnect.co.ke>

... in Southern Africa

Contact Anriette Esterhuysen, Sangonet, Johannesburg, South Africa.
E-mail: <anriette@sn.apc.org>

... in Latin America

Contact Erika Smith, APC Women's Networking Support Program at Laneta, Mexico.
E-mail: <erika@laneta.apc.org>

... in S.E. Asia

Contact: Roberto Verzola, Asialink Network, Manila, Philippines.
E-mail: <rverzola@phil.gn.apc.org>
Contact: Rhona Bautista or Pi Villanueva, ISIS, Manila, Philippines.
E-mail: <isis@phil.gn.apc.org> or <isis@mnl.sequel.net>

... in South Asia

Contact Swatija Paranjapa, Forum Against Oppression of Women (FAOW), Bombay, India.
E-mail: <admin@faow.ilbom.ernet.in> or <inforum@giasbm01.vsnl.net.in>
Contact: Leo Fernandez at Indialink, New Delhi, India.
E-mail: <leo@unv.ernet.in>

APC CONFERENCES ON WOMEN'S HUMAN RIGHTS

If you are part of the Association for Progressive Communications (APC) network, these are some of the conferences in which you can participate. The issues that these conferences cover may overlap but the individual articles may not, so it is beneficial to have a look at all of them. If you are not part of the APC network, send an e-mail to the conferences through Karen Banks in London, England, at: <karenb@gn.apc.org>.

WOMEN.NEWS

News, action alerts, articles and discussions relating to women's human rights.
E-mail: <women.news@conf.igc.apc.org>

HR.WOMEN

News, articles, action alerts focusing on women's human rights.
E-mail: <hr.women@conf.igc.apc.org>

HRNET.WOMEN

More articles on women's human rights.
E-mail: <hrnet.women@conf.igc.apc.org>

WOMEN.VIOLENCE

News, articles, action alerts and discussions focusing on violence against women.
E-mail: <women.violence@conf.igc.apc.org>

DH. MUJER

Information on women's human rights in Mexico and Central America, in Spanish and Portuguese.
E-mail: <women media@conf.igc.apc.org> →

USING INFORMATION TOOLS

Creating your own electronic list or conference

If there is no existing list or conference that focuses on your issues, you may want to start your own. First, contact groups in your network to find out who has access to e-mail and who does not and to see which Internet or network service provider they use. If all members use the same e-mail network service provider, you may be able to start a conference within that service. If the groups you are trying to link together use too many different network service providers, it might be wiser to use a list instead. In deciding whether a list or conference would best serve your needs, think of the advantages and potential disadvantages of both.

Translate information into more than one language where possible. The IWTC Women's GlobalNet, a bi-weekly one-page bulletin on initiatives and activites of women worldwide, is currently being sent out to two separate lists, one in English and one in Spanish. A third list in French is planned for Francophone Africa, Caribbean and Asia.

ELECTRONIC LISTS

ADVANTAGES	POTENTIAL DISADVANTAGES
• **QUICK.** Messages are usually sent and received instantly. While in some places there is a delay in receiving them, it's usually not more than a day or so.	• **EXPENSIVE.** Everyone on the list receives every message; this can get expensive for those who have to pay for every piece of information they receive.
• **COST-EFFECTIVE.** Usually, for the price of a local call, you can send the message to however many addresses on the list. Some networks charge gateway fees when e-mailing certain countries, but these still cost less than sending faxes.	• **NO RECORDS.** When you join a list, you cannot see the messages sent before you joined.
• **ACCESSIBLE.** Lists use e-mail, the most common and widely used form of electronic communications.	• **IMPERSONAL.** The same message is sent to everyone; you cannot personalize information. Also, electronic lists can be extensive and it's possible that you won't know all of the organizations that are receiving your information.
• **INCLUSIVE.** Anyone who can send and receive e-mail can participate.	• **INFORMATION OVERLOAD.** Unless the list has certain rules about message length, you may have too much information and not be able to read all of it.

AMLAT.MUJERES
News, in Spanish and Portuguese, on women's issues and events in Latin America and the Caribbean.
E-mail: <@amlat.mujeres>

UN.CSW.DOCS
UN Commission on the Status of Women documents and reports, as well as reports from the Committee on Elimination of Discrimination Against Women (CEDAW).
E-mail: <un.csw.docs@conf.igc.apc.org>

TAKING ACTION

USING INFORMATION TOOLS

ELECTRONIC CONFERENCES

Create a text-only version of your World Wide Web site. Users without high-speed modems will then still be able to receive the information but won't have to wait to download the graphics. For help, visit the Accessible HTML Guidelines: ‹http://pantheon.yale.edu/~nakamura/accessibility.html›.

ADVANTAGES	POTENTIAL DISADVANTAGES
• **INCLUSIVE.** Because the information goes to a central place or bulletin board, it can be accessed by all the members of the electronic network on which the conference is found. Any member can have input and all members can read and reply to that input. • **RECORD-KEEPING.** All of the messages are stored. The conference therefore acts as an archive. • **COST-EFFECTIVE.** For those who have to pay for every e-mail they receive, a conference is more cost effective than a list. Members can read and retrieve just the information they are interested in, rather than having to receive every message sent to the list. • **A FORUM OF LIKE-MINDED PEOPLE.** An electronic conference can "break the isolation" of activists worldwide, at the same time keeping them informed around specific issues.	• **EXCLUSIVE.** The information is only accessible to people who are members of that particular electronic network or service, for example the Association for Progressive Communications (APC) network. However, anyone with an e-mail account, no matter which network service provider she uses, can participate in an electronic list. (To solve this you could attach a mailing list of any e-mail addresses to the conference. Ask your network service provider how to do this.) • **REQUIRES ACTION.** Messages do not come directly to mailboxes. You must seek out the conference and look through the messages. • **PUBLIC FORUM.** While the outreach of conferences can be positive, they are a public forum and therefore sensitive information cannot be posted. (You can create a "closed" conference to share sensitive information. Contact the network provider to see how to do this.)

Once you've decided to start a list or conference, contact your network service provider for help with the initial set-up. In the case of a list, you will need to provide it with a list of addresses. You will also need to think about whether your list will be public and open to everyone or only open to certain people. You can choose whether you want messages to go straight to the list or to a moderator (the person who manages the technical aspects of the list, adds new names, troubleshoots problems, etc.) who "okays" the information first.

If you want your list to reach as wide an audience as possible, add the addresses of electronic conferences in addition to the names of groups or individuals to the mailing list so that the information will reach more people. For example, you can e-mail the address <women.violence@conf.igc.apc.org> or <hrnet.women@conf.igc.apc.org> to reach the 25 electronic networks that are members of the global APC electronic network.

116 RIGHTS OF WOMEN

USING INFORMATION TOOLS

Establish guidelines for your list or conference. You might want to set a one-page limit on messages to avoid information overload or unnecessary expense. Decide on the topics and questions to be considered to keep the discussions "on track." Also give people instructions on how to send mail to the list or messages and "netiquette"—guidelines about what are or are not appropriate kinds of interactions.

Create a digest or summary for newcomers to the list to catch them up on what's happened to date.

Send regular messages to the list or conference. Often it can take time to get a discussion going, especially if the people do not know each other very well. Posting regularly reminds and encourages people to become involved.

"How can I keep my messages private? I don't want everyone in the world reading everything I write on my computer!"

IS E-MAIL SECURE AND PRIVATE?

For many human right's activists this question is critical. The answer is no. E-mail can be intercepted by governments or others with the knowledge to do so. But by using certain tools, such as encryption or anonymous communications, electronic communications can be very secure—more secure than telephone, fax or postal mail.

Encryption is a way to scramble a message so that it makes no sense to the reader until she unscrambles it using a "key" or secret password. International Pretty Good Privacy (PGP) is free encryption software: <http://www.pgpi.com/>.

With an **anonymous remailer**, programme e-mail (anonymizer) can be sent with the sender's identity disguised.

Web sites:

Try <http://www.well.com/user/abacard/remail.html> and/or <http://www.anonymizer.com>

FACT

Time is a very important consideration for most people. How much time does it take to moderate an electronic conference or list?

This depends on how often you post or send information to the list and how much information filtering you do. Moderating a list can take anywhere from a few hours a week to a few days a week or more.

USING INFORMATION TOOLS

2 RECORD INFORMATION

"I'm going to document everything that happened to my daughter and take it to a lawyer."

> You can receive the text of any Web page via e-mail using "getweb." Send a message to: ‹getweb@ecn.cz› with the body of the message containing your request (the address of the page you want). The Web address must begin with ‹http://›.

Documenting women's human rights violations is crucial for a number of reasons. It exposes abuses that for too long have gone unnoticed. It brings much-needed attention to and pressure on those countries that continue to ignore violations against women. It enables activists to bring complaints to the appropriate United Nations committees, all of whom require specific evidence and details about any violations. Finally, accurate documentation requires countries to respond concretely to both specific instances of violations and long-term patterns of abuse.

Computer databases have been an unparalleled boon for people who document women's human rights violations. Thanks to standard database formats developed by networks such as the Canada-US Human Rights Information and Documentation Network (CUSHRIDNet), violations are now far easier to search and share. When immediate action is needed, the ability to speedily share accurate reports of violations can be life-saving.

Databases enable groups to document information about the victim of a violation, when and where the violation took place and who the perpetrator was. Each piece of information is entered into a specific area within the database known as a database field. A database may include any number of fields, such as name of victim, location of event and source of information.

One member of CUSHRIDNet, the Human Rights Information and Documentation Systems Inter-national (HURIDOCS), has defined a set of standard database formats so that human rights activists all over the globe can use the same types of fields. Standard formats do not require that all organizations use all the fields for all situations. Instead, they can be adapted or used selectively to fit individual needs. Anyone with access to the Internet can access these formats, or you can write to HURIDOCS for a copy of *HURIDOCS Standard Formats: A Tool for Documenting Human Rights Violations*, as well as its database software called EVSYS.

USING INFORMATION TOOLS

To start documenting women's human rights violations, these contacts could be very useful:

HUMAN RIGHTS INFORMATION AND DOCUMENTATION SYSTEMS INTERNATIONAL (HURIDOCS)
Any organization that would like to use HURIDOCS database formats to document cases of human rights violations can request a copy of its software, called EVSYS, from the HURIDOCS secretariat.
Address: 2 rue Jean-Jaquet
CH-1201 Geneva, Switzerland
Tel: 41-22-7411767
Fax: 41-22-7411768
E-mail: <huridocs@oln.comlink.apc.org>
Web site: <http://photon-63.iprolink.ch/~huridocs>

CUSHRIDNET
This network brings together those engaged in human rights documentation and information work to share information and explore ideas. It promotes uniform standards for human rights documentation, information management and exchange; and improving ties with information and documentation networks in other parts of the world. Based in North America, its outreach is global.
Contact: Ria Galanos
Address: AAAS, 1200 New York Avenue, NW, Washington, DC 20005, USA
Tel: (202) 326-6600
E-mail: <cushrid@aaas.org>
Web site: <http://shr.aaas.org/cushrid.htm>

COALITION AGAINST TRAFFICKING AGAINST WOMEN-ASIA PACIFIC
The coalition organizes training courses on using computers to systematically document cases of violence against women.
Address: Suite 406, Victoria Plaza, 41 Annapolis Street, Greenhills, San Juan, 1500 Metro Manila, Philippines
Tel: 63-2-722-0859
Fax: 62-3-722-0755
E-mail: <a.dedios@phil.gn.apc.org>

WOMEN'S HUMAN RIGHTS, STEP BY STEP
This book, published by the Women, Law & Development International and Human Rights Watch Women's Rights Project, includes excellent instructions for investigating and documenting human rights abuses—with or without a computer database. Available from: Women, Ink.
Address: 777 United Nations Plaza, New York, NY 10017, USA
Tel: 1-212-687 8633
Fax: 1-212-661 2704
E-mail: <wink@womenink.org>
Web site: <http://www.womenink.org>

Set up an auto-mailing list of documents to increase availability of documents to e-mail only users.

Ask your network service provider for instructions.

HURIDOCS
HUMAN RIGHTS INFORMATION AND DOCUMENTATION SYSTEMS

Standard Database Format

RECORDING AN EVENT*

Field name:	data
Event Record Number:	E004
Geographical Term:	Zimbabwe
Type of Event:	Disappearance
Initial Date:	19850131
Type of Location:	Communal area

Perpetrator Remarks:

The abductors were well-fed and well-dressed. They pretended to be from a particular ethnic group but it was obvious that they could not speak that language. Their vehicles made the same sound as those used by local police. There are no vehicles in the area except on the mission and at the Police Camp.

*Not a real record. This is only an example of a possible record of an event.

A Guided Tour of Women's

STOP 1 [TO] = text-only version available [L] = links to other resources

Women's Human Rights Advocates

Women, Law & Development International [TO, L]. Organizational information programmes, projects and publications that aim to expand rights, education and legal literacy among women. The site also has excellent links to other women's rights resources.
Web site: <http://www.wld.org>

Center for Women's Global Leadership-1998 Global Campaign [L]. The 1998 Global Campaign seeks to provide public education tools that can be used by local, national, regional and international organizations to highlight women's human rights. This site provides links and activities. It is available through gopher as well as the World Wide Web.
Web site: <http://www-rci.rutgers.edu/~cwgl/humanrights> or <gopher://gopher.igc.apc.org:70/11/orgs/cwgl>

The Global Alliance Against Traffic in Women Updates on global action around the traffic and migration of women and protection of their human rights with an Asia-Pacific focus.
Web site: <http://www.inet.co.th/org/gaatw>

African Human Rights Resource Centre A joint project of the Makerere Human Rights and Peace Centre and the University of Minnesota Human Rights Center, this page contains a collection of international human rights materials with a particular focus on Africa. The site also includes information about ratification of international human rights treaties, information on the International Criminal Tribunal for Rwanda, as well as information about NGOs in Sub-Saharan Africa.
Web site: <http://www.umn.edu/humanrts/africa/index.html>

SYNFEV-Synergy Gender and Development is the woman-and-gender-focused component of ENDA (Environment and Development Action in the Third World). The organization is based in Dakar, Senegal, and works in partnership with the associations, groups and networks active in the same fields: economics, health, violence and communication for women. Its Web site is bilingual (French and English).
Web site: <http:www.enda.sn/synfev/synfev.htm>

Budi aktivna Budi emancipirana—Be Active Be Emancipated (BaBe). This women's human rights education workshop focuses on women's rights in Croatia.
Web site: <http://www.interlog.com/~moyra>

Women Living Under Muslim Laws Network This is a network of 30 women's groups in regions where women live under Muslim law.
E-mail: wluml@mail.mnet.fr

Equality Now An active group of women in New York that monitors and acts on women's rights violations globally. Action alerts are its main tool.
Web site: www.equalitynow.org/brochure_eng_hub.html

Human Rights Watch: Women's Rights Project [L] This global report on women's rights seeks to investigate and expose human rights violations and hold abusers accountable. It challenges governments and those who hold power to end abusive practices and respect international human rights law and it enlists the public and the international community to support the cause of human rights for all. It has divisions in Africa, the Americas, Asia, Europe and the Middle East.
Web site: <http://www.hrw.org/about/projects/women.html> or <gopher://gopher.igc.apc.org:5000/11/int/hrw/women>

Amnesty International—USA Women's Human Rights Program Contains information about Amnesty International as well as specific action alerts.
Web site: <http://www.igc.apc.org/amnesty/women/index.html>

Womensnet Electronic Network Facilitates conferences covering many issues among women worldwide and sends out human rights news and developments as well as action alerts.
Web site: <http://www.igc.org/igc/womensnet>

The Global Fund for Women A comprehensive Web site that gives funding guidelines and information on women's human rights, women's access to media and communication technology and women's economic autonomy.
Web site: <http://www.igc.apc.org/gfw>

STOP 4

Country Reports & International Law

University of Minnesota Human Rights Library. This site provides human rights information by country as well as international law. It also includes UN documents and conventions.
Web site: <http://www.umn.edu/humanrts/index.html>

International Centre for Human Rights and Democratic Development. This centre provides information on women's rights in Africa, the Americas and Asia and can be accessed in either English or French.
Web site: <http://www.ichrdd.ca> or <gopher://gopher.igc.apc.org:70/11/orgs/ichrdd>

Internet Resources for Women's Legal and Public Policy Information [L]. This site provides links to women's legal resources within the United States and internationally.
Web site:
<http://asa.ugl.lib.umich.edu/chdocs/womenpolicy/womenlawpolicy.html>

Human Rights On-line Communities

STOP 2
UN Human Rights Bodies and Conventions

United Nations Human Rights Bodies Here you will find the Universal Declaration of Human Rights and the International Criminal Tribunal for the Former Yugoslavia (ICTY). Web site: <http://www.un.org/rights>

United Nations Commission on Human Rights This easy-to-navigate site also includes the Universal Declaration of Human Rights as well as country reports and a guide to the UN human rights committees. Web site: <http://www.unhchr.ch>

The UN Division for the Advancement of Women (UN/DAW),
UN Development Fund for Women (UNIFEM), and
UN Inter. Research & Training Inst. for the Advancement of Women (INSTRAW), all collaborate in *WomenWatch: The UN Internet Gateway for the Advancement and Empowerment of Women*. Originally set up to support the implementation of the Beijing Platform for Action, WomenWatch contains many women's rights documents and reports. These include: CEDAW, official documents of sessions of Commission on the Status of Women (CSW) and National Plans of Action and Strategies.
Web site: <http://www.un.org./womenwatch>. E-mail: <womenwatch@un.org>

UN Development Fund for Women (UNIFEM) [L] UNIFEM has a special section on its own web site for UNIFEM human rights publications and activities, plus relevant UN Conventions and other documents. This site is linked to *Women, Ink.,* which is the exclusive distributor of UNIFEM materials.
Web-site: <www.unifem.undp.org>. E-mail: <unifem@undp.org>

The UN Division for the Advancement of Women (UN/DAW) has its own web site also, and as the secretariat for CEDAW and the CSW, this site contains additional documentation for these UN bodies.
Web site: <www.un.org/dpcsd/daw>. E-mail: daw@un.org>

STOP 3
Human Rights Resource and Documentation Centres

DIANA: International Human Rights Database of Women's Human Rights Resources [L]. This is an annotated listing of sites for legal research in women's international human rights by category; also an annotated bibliography of women's human rights documents including conventions, reports, bibliographies and articles of governmental and non-governmental organizations.
Web site: <http://www.law-lib.utoronto.ca/diana>

Human Rights Internet [L]. HRI is in contact with more than five thousand organizations and individuals working for the advancement of human rights worldwide. HRI includes a searchable database on human rights organizations, literature, funding and awards as well as education resources.
Web site: <http://www.hri.ca>

Human Rights Information Sources on the Internet [L]. This is a database of human rights Internet sites. It also includes an index of electronic publications, tools and resources for using the Internet and a human rights research helpline.
Web site: <http://shr.aaas.org/dhr.htm>

Human Rights Web: Human Rights Organizations and Resources [L]. This page contains names and links to human rights organizations and resources helpful to human rights activists and researchers. Resources are listed either internationally or regionally.
Web site: <http://www.hrweb.org/resource.html>

Partners in Human Rights Education. This is an annotated bibliography of women's human rights education resources, including books and education packages. Web site:
<http://www.umn.edu/humanrts/education/pihre/women.htm>

People's Decade for Human Rights Education. PDHRE works directly and indirectly with its network of affiliates — primarily women's and social justice organizations — to develop and advance pedagogies for human rights education. Projects include the development of human rights education manuals and publications, and the setting up of Human Rights Communities. Its Web site links with many other human rights groups.
Web site: <http://www.pdhre.org>
E-mail: <pdhre@igc.apc.org>

TAKING ACTION **121**

USING INFORMATION TOOLS

3 PRODUCE INFORMATION

FACT

When you visit a Web site, you leave a calling card that reveals where you're coming from and what kind of computer you have.

With all the information available in electronic mailing lists, conferences, World Wide Web sites and other electronic spaces, electronic tools are frequently used only for finding and receiving human rights information. But one of greatest advantages of the Internet is that it enables us to produce and publish human rights information.

There are a number of ways to use computers to produce information. Two of these are desktop publishing and Web publishing. Used alone or in combination, both are rapidly changing how and where we publish. Desktop publishing, which requires a computer and printer, allows groups to produce bulletins, newsletters and alerts so that they are ready for printing, saving both time and money. With Web publishing—which requires a computer, a modem to directly access the Internet, HTML and Web browser software—we can now produce on-line newsletters that can be accessed by thousands—even millions—without a printing press. With both types of publishing, text and graphics can be shared either over the Internet or on a computer disk, making the information more adaptable to a specific situation or need.

"I don't have to cut and paste with glue and scissors anymore. I can do the newsletter on my computer."

Become your own desktop publisher

No longer such a "new" technology, desktop publishing (DTP) uses a computer, page layout software, a laser printer and other equipment such as scanners (to scan graphics onto a computer) to create publication pages that are camera-ready or ready to print. Action alerts and brochures, human rights training manuals and information booklets are just some of the highly effective materials that can be made using DTP.

Although DTP can be very "high tech"—very expensive combinations of software and hardware that create printed pages with all the graphics in place are now available—DTP can also be low-tech. Using basic software and a standard printer, text-only pages can be produced and graphics added by hand. And because the information is created electronically, it can also be shared electronically via a computer disk.

122 RIGHTS OF WOMEN

USING INFORMATION TOOLS

Web publishing

For those activists who have modems and access to the World Wide Web, the ability to present text, graphics, audio or video on Web pages and to link users to other electronic resources makes Web publishing an effective, engaging means for reaching many people globally. Unfortunately, because it works best with a high-speed modem (28,800 bps or higher) and direct Internet access, Web publishing remains one of the more inaccessible tools. So whether you should try Web publishing depends on your resources, your country's infrastructure and telecommunications set-up and, most importantly, who it is you want to reach: Do <u>they</u> have access to the Web?

Web pages are created with computer software that uses hypertext markup language (HTML) and a Web browser (a programme that lets your computer read Web sites).

As mentioned above, accessing the Web requires a high-speed modem and a computer with lots of memory because the data files are large and take time to be processed.

So, to decide whether Web publishing makes sense for your group, consider the following questions: What is the goal of your Web site. Is it to inform? Persuade?

Why would a Web site be a better vehicle than other forms of publishing?

Think about who you are trying to reach. Is it the people with whom you work? Is it other human rights organizations? Maybe it's funding agencies? Or country leaders? Do all of them have access to the Web?

Do you have staff with the skills needed to build and maintain your Web site or will you have to hire someone else to do it for you? How much control do you want over changes and format? How will you respond to increased correspondence that often comes with a Web site? Devise a rough work plan to help you estimate your staff needs. The plan should include each task to be done, the person to do it and the estimated time and cost. Besides writing the content and designing the graphics, think about how you will advertise the site.

If your group or network decides that a Web site is both powerful and practical for your human rights work, you can consult any of the resources on the next page.

FACT

The symbols ‹ › are not part of the Internet address itself. They show you where an address begins and ends.

USING INFORMATION TOOLS

BOOKS

ACCESSING THE INTERNET: A PRIMER FOR HUMAN RIGHTS ORGANIZATIONS AND INDIVIDUALS
Stephen Hansen, AAAS
Science and Human Rights Program, American Association for the Advancement of Science, 1200 New York Avenue, NW, Washington, DC 20005, **USA**
Tel: (202) 326-6790
Fax: (202) 289-4950
E-mail: ‹shansen@aaas.org›

THE ESSENTIAL INTERNET: BASICS FOR INTERNATIONAL NGOS
Carlos Parada and Janet Green, InterAction, Washington, 1997
This is also a thorough resource for organizations thinking about starting a Web site. Available through InterAction, American Council for Voluntary International Action, 1717 Massachusetts Avenue NW, Suite 801, Washington, DC 20036, **USA**
Tel: (202) 667-8227
Fax: (202) 667-8236
E-mail: ‹ia@interaction.org›
Web site: ‹http://www.interaction.org›

WOMEN'S GUIDE TO THE WIRED WORLD
Shana Penn, 1997
A guide to the Internet and electronic networking for women that covers: e-mail lists, navigating the Web, on-line research, etc. Includes an extensive listing of electronic resources organized by subject.
and
WOW: WOMEN ON THE WEB
Helen Fallon, 1997
Includes internet addresses for electronic conferences, bibliographies, library catalogues, research centres, etc. Also has a beginner's guide to setting up a home page.

Both books available from Women, Ink., (contact information on pages 146-8).

RESOURCES

FINDING, USING AND PUBLISHING HUMAN RIGHTS INFORMATION ON THE INTERNET
This on-line guide covers tips for finding, using and publishing human rights information on the Internet. It includes information on the history of the Internet, how to create your own home page, resources, search engines and directories.
Web site:
‹http://www.aaas.org/spp/dspp/shr/net-shop.html›

CREATING A SUCCESSFUL WEB PAGE
Contains detailed steps on how to create, maintain and modify your own Web site.
Web site:
‹http://www.hooked.net/wenet/support/website.html›

LIBRARY AND INFORMATION TECHNOLOGY ASSOCIATION 15 MINUTE SERIES
The 15 Minute Series is a collection of Internet training materials designed to assist members of the research and education community to incorporate the Internet in their day-to-day operations and activities. The training materials are educational and immediately usable.
Web site: ‹http://www.rs.internic.net/nic-support/15min›

THE INTERNET ROADMAP 1996
Roadmap 96 is a 27-lesson, text-based Internet training workshop designed to teach new "Net travelers" how to travel around the rapidly expanding (and often confusing) "Information Superhighway."
Web site: ‹http://www.rs.internic.net/nic-support/roadmap96›

INTERNET GLOSSARY
An extensive glossary of Internet-related terms to help you understand the language of the Internet.
Web site:
‹http://www.matisse.net/files/glossary.html›

MAIDEN-L
Discussion group for women. To subscribe:
Web site: ‹majordomo@women.ca›
Message: ‹subscribe maiden-l›

5

Resource Kit

IN THIS SECTION

- Convention Abbreviations Used in Ratification Charts
- Ratification Charts
- UN Human Rights Conventions Chart
- CEDAW
- Anatomy of the Platform for Action
- About IWTC and Women, Ink.
- Women, Ink. Resources and Order Form

Ratification Charts: Convention Abbreviations

UN Human Rights Conventions

ICCPR .... International Covenant on Civil and Political Rights

OPICCPR ...... Optional Protocol to International Covenant on Civil and Political Rights

ICESCR .... International Covenant on Economic, Social and Cultural Rights

CEDAW .... Convention on the Elimination of All Forms of Discrimination Against Women

ICERD .... International Convention on the Elimination of All Forms of Racial Discrimination

CRC .... Convention on the Rights of the Child

CDE .... Convention against Discrimination in Education

ERC .... Equal Remuneration Convention

MPC .... Maternity Protection Convention

DC .... Discrimination (Employment and Occupation) Convention

WFRC .... Workers with Family Responsibilities Convention

HWC* .... Home Work Convention (not yet entered into force)

CNMW .... Convention on the Nationality of Married Women

CCM .... Convention on Consent to Marriage, Minimum Age for Marriage and Registration of Marriage

CRSR .... Convention Relating to the Status of Refugees/Protocol Relating to the Status of Refugees

CSTPEP .... Convention for the Suppression of the Traffic in Persons and the Exploitation of the Prostitution of Others

SCAS .... Supplemtary Convention on the Abolition of Slavery, the Slave Trade and Institutions and Practices Similar to Slavery

CAT .... Convention Against Torture and Other Cruel, Inhuman or Degrading Treatment or Punishment

UN Human Rights Conventions

Africa
(Ratifications as of May 31, 1997)

	ICCPR	OPICCPR	ICESCR	CEDAW	ICERD	CRC	CDE	ERC	MPC	DC	WFRC	HWC*	CNMW	CCM	CRSR	CSTPEP	SCAS	CAT
Algeria	R	R	R	R	R	R	R	R		R					R	R	R	R
Angola	R	R	R	R	R	R	R	R		R					R		R	
Benin	R	R	R	R		R	R	R		R				R	R	R		R
Botswana					R	R									R			
Burkina Faso				R	R	R	R	R		R				R	R	R		
Burundi	R		R	R	R	R	R	R		R					R	R	R	R
Cameroon	R	R	R	R	R	R	R	R		R					R	R		R
Cape Verde	R		R	R	R	R	R	R		R								R
Central African Republic	R	R	R	R	R	R	R	R		R					R	R	R	
Chad	R	R	R	R	R	R	R	R		R					R			R
Comoros				R		R												
Congo	R	R	R	R	R	R	R								R	R	R	
Cote d'Ivoire	R	R	R	R	R	R		R		R				R	R	R	R	R
Djibouti						R		R							R	R	R	
Egypt	R		R	R	R	R	R	R							R	R	R	R
Equatorial Guinea	R	R	R	R	R	R		R							R			
Ethiopia	R		R	R	R	R				R					R	R	R	R
Gabon	R		R	R	R	R		R		R					R			
Gambia	R	R		R	R	R				R			R		R	R		
Ghana	R		R	R	R	R	R	R		R				R	R	R	R	
Guinea	R	R	R	R	R	R			R	R	R				R		R	R
Guinea-Bissau			R	R	R	R				R					R		R	R
Kenya	R		R	R	R	R							R		R	R	R	
Lesotho	R		R	R	R	R	R	R							R			R
Liberia				R	R	R	R			R					R			
Libyan Arab Jamahiriya	R	R	R	R	R	R	R	R	R	R			R			R	R	R
Madagascar	R	R	R	R	R	R	R			R					R		R	

*Not Entered into Force
R = Ratified or Acceded

Africa
(Ratifications as of May 31, 1997)

	ICCPR	OPICCPR	ICESCR	CEDAW	ICERD	CRC	CDE	ERC	MPC	DC	WFRC	HWC*	CNMW	CCM	CRSR	CSTPEP	SCAS	CAT
Malawi	R		R	R	R	R		R		R			R		R	R	R	R
Mali	R		R	R	R	R		R		R			R	R	R	R	R	R
Mauritania					R	R				R					R	R	R	
Mauritius	R	R	R	R	R	R	R						R			R	R	R
Morocco	R		R	R	R	R	R	R							R		R	R
Mozambique	R			R	R	R		R							R			
Namibia	R	R	R	R	R	R												R
Niger	R	R	R	R	R	R	R			R				R	R	R	R	
Nigeria	R		R	R	R	R	R								R			
Rwanda	R		R	R	R	R				R					R			
Sao Tome & Principe						R				R					R			
Senegal	R	R	R	R	R	R	R	R		R					R	R	R	R
Seychelles	R	R	R	R	R	R									R	R	R	R
Sierra Leone	R	R	R	R		R	R	R		R			R		R	R	R	
Somalia	R	R	R		R		R			R								
South Africa				R		R								R	R	R		R
Sudan	R		R		R	R	R	R		R					R			
Swaziland					R	R	R	R		R			R				R	
Togo	R	R	R	R	R	R	R	R		R			R	R	R	R	R	R
Tunisia	R		R	R	R	R	R	R					R		R		R	R
Uganda	R	R	R	R	R	R	R	R		R			R		R		R	R
United Republic of Tanzania	R		R	R	R	R	R						R				R	
Zaire	R	R	R	R	R	R		R							R		R	R
Zambia	R	R	R	R	R	R		R	R	R					R		R	
Zimbabwe	R		R	R	R	R		R		R			R	R	R	R	R	

*Not Entered into Force
R = Ratified or Acceded

UN Human Rights Conventions

Asia
(Ratifications as of May 31, 1997)

	ICCPR	OP1CCPR	ICESCR	CEDAW	ICERD	CRC	CDE	ERC	MPC	DC	WFRC	HWC*	CNMW	CCM	CRSR	CSTPEP	SCAS	CAT
Afghanistan	R		R		R	R		R	R								R	R
Bangladesh				R	R	R		R	R							R	R	R
Bhutan				R		R												
Cambodia	R		R	R	R	R	R								R		R	R
China				R	R	R	R								R			
Democratic People's Rep. of Korea	R		R					R										
India	R		R	R	R	R	R	R	R							R	R	
Indonesia				R		R	R	R										
Iran	R		R		R	R	R		R						R	R	R	
Japan	R		R	R	R	R					R				R			
Lao People's Democratic Republic				R	R	R											R	
Malaysia				R	R	R	R						R					
Maldives		R		R	R	R	R										R	
Mongolia	R		R	R	R	R	R	R	R	R				R			R	R
Myanmar	R		R	R	R	R	R		R									
Nepal	R		R	R	R	R	R	R	R								R	R
Pakistan		R	R	R	R	R	R	R	R									
Philippines	R	R	R	R	R	R	R	R	R				R	R	R	R	R	R
Republic of Korea	R	R	R	R	R	R							R		R	R	R	R
Singapore				R		R												
Sri Lanka	R		R	R	R	R	R	R		R			R	R			R	
Thailand	R			R		R											R	
Viet Nam	R		R	R	R	R	R									R	R	R

*Not Entered into Force
R = Ratified or Acceded

Caribbean/North America

UN Human Rights Conventions

(Ratifications as of May 31, 1997)

	ICCPR	OPICCPR	ICESCR	CEDAW	ICERD	CRC	CDE	ERC	MPC	DC	WFRC	HWC*	CNMW	CCM	CRSR	CSTPEP	SCAS	CAT
Antigua & Barbuda				R	R	R				R			R	R	R		R	R
Bahamas				R	R	R							R	R	R		R	
Barbados	R	R	R	R	R	R	R	R		R			R	R			R	
Belize	R			R	R	R	R								R			R
Dominica	R		R	R	R	R	R			R					R		R	
Grenada	R		R	R	R	R												
Guyana	R	R	R	R	R	R				R								R
Jamaica	R	R	R	R	R	R		R		R			R		R		R	
St. Kitts & Nevis				R	R	R												
St. Lucia				R	R	R		R		R			R				R	
St Vincent & the Grenadines	R		R	R	R	R	R										R	
Suriname	R	R	R	R	R	R									R		R	
Trinidad & Tobago	R	R	R	R	R	R				R			R	R			R	
Canada	R	R	R	R	R	R		R		R			R		R			R
United States of America	R				R													R

*Not Entered into Force
R = Ratified or Acceded

UN Human Rights Conventions

Europe
(Ratifications as of May 31, 1997)

	ICCPR	OP1CCPR	ICESCR	CEDAW	ICERD	CRC	CDE	ERC	MPC	DC	WFRC	HWC*	CNMW	CCM	CRSR	CSTPEP	SCAS	CAT
Albania	R			R	R	R	R	R										R
Armenia	R	R	R	R	R	R	R	R					R		R	R	R	R
Austria	R	R	R	R	R	R	R	R		R			R	R	R		R	R
Azerbaijan	R			R	R	R		R	R	R			R		R	R	R	R
Belarus	R		R	R	R	R		R	R	R			R			R	R	R
Belgium	R		R	R	R	R	R	R	R	R					R	R	R	
Bosnia & Herzegovina	R	R	R	R	R	R	R	R		R	R		R	R	R	R	R	R
Bulgaria	R	R	R	R	R	R	R	R		R			R		R	R	R	R
Croatia	R	R	R	R	R	R	R	R	R	R	R		R	R	R	R	R	R
Cyprus	R	R	R	R	R	R	R	R		R			R	R	R	R	R	R
Czech Republic	R	R	R	R	R	R	R	R		R			R	R	R	R	R	R
Denmark	R	R	R	R	R	R	R	R	R	R			R	R	R		R	R
Estonia	R	R	R	R	R	R	R	R							R			R
Finland	R	R	R	R	R	R	R	R		R	R		R	R	R	R	R	R
France	R	R	R	R	R	R		R		R	R				R	R	R	R
Georgia	R	R	R	R		R	R	R		R					R			R
Germany	R		R	R	R	R	R	R	R	R			R	R	R		R	R
Greece			R	R	R	R	R	R	R	R	R				R			R
Holy See[1]					R	R									R			
Hungary	R	R	R	R	R	R	R	R		R			R	R	R	R	R	R
Iceland	R	R	R	R	R			R					R	R			R	R
Ireland	R	R	R	R	R	R		R		R			R				R	
Italy	R	R	R	R	R	R	R	R	R	R					R		R	R
Kazakhstan						R	R	R		R					R			
Kyrgyzstan	R	R	R	R	R	R	R	R		R			R	R	R	R		R
Latvia	R	R	R	R	R	R	R	R		R			R				R	R

*Not Entered into Force
R = Ratified or Acceded
[1] Not a UN member state

UN Human Rights Conventions

Europe
(Ratifications as of May 31, 1997)

	ICCPR	OPICCPR	ICESCR	CEDAW	ICERD	CRC	CDE	ERC	MPC	DC	WFRC	HWC*	CNMW	CCM	CRSR	CSTPEP	SCAS	CAT
Liechtenstein	R			R		R												R
Lithuania	R	R	R	R	R	R		R		R					R			R
Luxembourg	R	R	R	R	R	R	R	R	R				R		R	R	R	R
Malta	R	R	R	R	R	R	R	R	R	R			R		R		R	R
Monaco	R				R	R												R
Netherlands	R	R	R	R	R	R	R	R	R	R	R		R	R	R	R	R	R
Norway	R	R	R	R	R	R	R	R	R	R	R			R	R	R	R	R
Poland	R	R	R	R	R	R	R	R	R	R			R	R	R	R	R	R
Portugal	R	R	R	R	R	R	R	R	R	R	R				R	R	R	R
Republic of Moldova	R		R	R	R	R	R	R	R	R							R	R
Romania	R	R	R	R	R	R	R	R		R			R		R	R	R	R
Russian Federation	R	R	R	R	R	R	R	R		R			R		R	R	R	R
San Marino	R	R	R			R		R		R	R						R	
Slovak Republic	R	R	R	R	R	R	R	R	R	R	R		R	R	R	R	R	R
Slovenia	R	R	R	R	R	R	R	R	R	R	R		R	R	R	R	R	R
Spain	R	R	R	R	R	R	R	R	R	R	R			R	R	R	R	R
Sweden	R	R	R	R	R	R		R		R	R		R	R	R	R	R	R
Switzerland[1]	R			R	R			R	R	R					R			R
Tajikistan				R	R			R	R	R					R			
The Former Yugoslavia/ Rep. of Macedonia	R		R	R	R	R	R	R					R	R	R	R	R	
Turkey				R		R	R	R		R								R
Turkmenistan	R	R	R	R	R	R		R									R	
Ukraine	R	R	R	R	R	R	R	R	R	R			R	R	R	R	R	R
United Kingdom	R		R	R	R	R		R					R		R			R
Uzbekistan	R	R	R	R	R	R		R	R				D					R
Yugoslavia	R		R	R	R	R	R	R	R	R	R		R	R	R	R	R	R

*=Not Entered into Force R = Ratified or Acceded [1] =Not a UN member state

Latin America

(Ratifications as of May 31, 1997)

	ICCPR	OPICCPR	ICESCR	CEDAW	ICERD	CRC	CDE	ERC	MPC	DC	CEEO	HWC*	CNMW	CCM	CRSR	CSTPEP	SCAS	CAT
Argentina	R	R	R	R	R	R	R	R		R	R		R	R	R	R	R	R
Bolivia	R	R	R	R	R	R		R	R	R				R	R	R	R	R
Brazil	R		R	R	R	R	R	R	R¹	R			R	R	R	R	R	R
Chile	R			R	R	R	R	R	R	R	R				R		R	R
Colombia	R	R	R	R	R	R		R		R					R			
Costa Rica	R	R	R	R	R	R	R	R		R					R		R	R
Cuba				R	R	R	R	R	R	R			R	R		R	R	R
Dominican Republic	R	R	R	R	R	R	R	R		R			R	R	R		R	R
Ecuador	R	R	R	R	R	R	R	R	R	R			R		R	R	R	R
El Salvador	R	R	R	R	R	R		R		R					R			R
Guatemala	R		R	R	R	R	R	R	R	R	R		R	R	R		R	R
Haiti	R			R	R	R		R	R	R					R		R	R
Honduras		S	R	R		R		R		R						R		R
Mexico	R		R	R	R	R	R	R		R			R	R		R	R	R
Nicaragua	R	R	R	R	R	R	R	R		R			R		R		R	
Panama	R	R	R	R	R	R	R	R		R					R			
Paraguay	R	R	R	R		R		R		R					R			
Peru	R	R	R	R	R	R	R	R		R	R				R	R		R
Uruguay	R	R	R	R	R	R		R	R	R	R				R		R	R
Venezuela	R	R	R	R	R	R	R	R	D	R	R		R	R		R	R	R

*Not Entered into Force
R = Ratified or Acceded   D = Denounced
¹With the exception of the occupations and work specified in Art. 7 para 1 (b) and (c)

UN Human Rights Conventions

Pacific
(Ratifications as of May 31, 1997)

	ICCPR	OPICCPR	ICESCR	CEDAW	ICERD	CRC	CDE	ERC	MPC	DC	WFRC	HWC*	CNMW	CCM	CRSR	CSTPEP	SCAS	CAT
Australia	R	R	R	R	R	R	R	R		R	R		R		R		R	R
Fiji				R	R	R							R	R	R		R	
Kiribati[1]						R												
Marshall Islands						R												
Micronesia/ Federated States of						R												
Nauru						R												
New Zealand	R	R	R	R	R	R	R	R		R			R	R	R		R	R
Papua New Guinea				R	R	R									R			
Samoa				R		R								R	R			
Solomon Islands			R		R	R	R								R		R	
Tonga[1]					R	R												
Tuvalu[1]						R									R			
Vanuatu				R		R												R

*Not Entered into Force
R = Ratified or Acceded
[1] Not a UN member state

UN Human Rights Conventions

Western Asia

(Ratifications as of May 31, 1997)

	ICCPR	OP1CCPR	ICESCR	CEDAW	ICERD	CRC	CDE	ERC	MPC	DC	WFRC	HWC*	CNMW	CCM	CRSR	CSTPEP	SCAS	CAT
Bahrain						R												
Brunei Darussalem						R	R										R	
Iraq	R		R	R	R	R	R	R		R						R	R	R
Israel	R		R	R	R	R	R	R		R			R		R	R	R	R
Jordan	R		R	R	R	R	R	R		R			R	R		R	R	R
Kuwait	R		R	R	R	R	R			R							R	
Lebanon	R		R		R	R	R	R		R								
Oman						R												
Qatar					R	R				R								
Saudi Arabia						R	R	R		R							R	
Syrian Arab Republic	R		R		R	R		R		R						R	R	
United Arab Emirates					R	R												
Yemen	R		R	R	R	R	R	R		R				R	R	R		R

*Not Entered into Force
R = Ratified or Acceded

UN HUMAN RIGHTS CONVENTIONS: DOCUMENT N°/WHEN ADOPTED/ENTERED INTO FORCE/RATIFIED

ACRONYM	NAME OF CONVENTION	DOCUMENT NO.	ADOPTED	ENTERED INTO FORCE	RATIFICATION (No. of countries)
ICCPR	International Covenant on Civil and Political Rights	2200A(XXI)	16 December 1966	23 March 1976	133
OPICCPR	Optional Protocol to the International Covenant on Civil and Political Rights	2200A (XXI)	16 December 1966	23 March 1976	87
ICESCR	International Covenant on Economic, Social and Cultural Rights	2200A(XXI)	16 December 1966	3 January 1976	134
CEDAW	Convention on the Elimination of all Forms of Discrimination against Women	34/180	18 December 1979	3 September 1981	153
ICERD	International Convention on the Elimination of All Forms of Racial Discrimination	2106A(XX)	21 December 1965	4 January 1969	146
CRC	Convention on the Rights of the Child	A/RES/44/25	20 November 1989	2 September 1990	187
CDE	Convention against Discrimination in Education	429 U.N.T.S. 93	14 December 1960	22 May 1962	85
ERC	Equal Remuneration Convention	C.100	29 June 1951	23 May 1953	126
MPC	Maternity Protection Convention (Revised)	C.103	4 June 1952	7 September 1955	34
DC	Discrimination (Employment and Occupation) Convention	C.111	24 June 1958	15 June 1960	122
WFRC	Workers with Family Responsibilities Convention	C.156	June 1981	11 August 1983	25
HWC	Home Work Convention	C.177	June 1996	Not Entered into Force	0
CNMW	Convention on the Nationality of Married Women	1040(XI)1	29 January 1957	11 August 1958	64
CCM	Convention on Consent to Marriage, Minimum Age for Marriage and Registration of Marriages	521 U.N.T.S. 231	7 November 1962	9 December 1964	45
CSR	Convention Relating to the Status of Refugees	189 U.N.T.S. 150	28 July 1951	22 April 1954	127
CSTPEP	Convention for the Suppression of the Traffic in Person and of the Exploitation of the Prostitution of Others	96 U.N.T.S. 271	2 December 1949	25 July 1951	70
SCAS	Supplementary Convention on the Abolition of Slavery, the Slave Trade, and Institutions and Practices Similar to Slavery	226 U.N.T.S. 3	30 April 1956	30 April 1957	114
CAT	Convention against Torture and Other Cruel, Inhuman or Degrading Treatment or Punishment	39/46	10 December 1984	26 June 1987	96

CONVENTION ON THE ELIMINATION OF ALL FORMS OF DISCRIMINATION AGAINST WOMEN

"...the full and complete development of a country, the welfare of the world and the cause of peace require the maximum participation of women on equal terms with men in all fields."

PREAMBLE

The States Parties to the present Convention,

Noting that the Charter of the United Nations reaffirms faith in fundamental human rights, in the dignity and worth of the human person and in the equal rights of men and women,

Noting that the Universal Declaration of Human Rights affirms the principle of the inadmissibility of discrimination and proclaims that all human beings are born free and equal in dignity and rights and that everyone is entitled to all the rights and freedoms set forth therein, without distinction of any kind, including distinction based on sex,

Noting that the States Parties to the International Covenants on Human Rights have the obligation to ensure the equal right of men and women to enjoy all economic, social, cultural, civil and political rights,

Considering the international conventions concluded under the auspices of the United Nations and the specialized agencies promoting equality of rights of men and women,

Noting also the resolutions, declarations and recommendations adopted by the United Nations and the specialized agencies promoting equality of rights of men and women,

Concerned, however, that despite these various instruments extensive discrimination against women continues to exist,

Recalling that discrimination against women violates the principles of equality of rights and respect for human dignity, is an obstacle to the participation of women, on equal terms with men, in the political, social, economic and cultural life of their countries, hampers the growth of the prosperity of society and the family and makes more difficult the full development of the potentialities of women in the service of their countries and of humanity,

Concerned that in situations of poverty women have the least access to food, health, education, training and opportunities for employment and other needs,

Convinced that the establishment of the new international economic order based on equity and justice will contribute significantly towards the promotion of equality between men and women,

Emphasizing that the eradication of apartheid, of all forms of racism, racial discrimination, colonialism, neo-colonialism, aggression, foreign occupation and domination and interference in the internal affairs of States is essential to the full enjoyment of the rights of men and women,

Affirming that the strengthening of international peace and security, relaxation of international tension, mutual co-operation among all States irrespective of their social and economic systems, general and complete disarmament, and in particular nuclear disarmament under strict and effective international control, the affirmation of the principles of justice, equality and mutual benefit in relations among countries and the realization of the right of peoples under alien and colonial domination and foreign occupation to self-determination and independence, as well as respect for national sovereignty and territorial integrity, will promote social progress and development and as a consequence will contribute to the attainment of full equality between men and women,

Convinced that the full and complete development of a country, the welfare of the world and the cause of peace require the maximum participation of women on equal terms with men in all fields,

Bearing in mind the great contribution of women to the welfare of the family and to the development of society, so far not fully recognized, the social significance of maternity and the role of both parents in the family and in the upbringing of children, and aware that the role of women in procreation should not be a basis for discrimination but that the upbringing of children requires a sharing of responsibility between men and women and society as a whole,

Aware that a change in the traditional role of men as well as the role of women in society and in the family is needed to achieve full equality between men and women,

Determined to implement the principles set forth in the Declaration on the Elimination of Discrimination Against Women and, for that purpose, to adopt the measures required for the elimination of such discrimination in all its forms and manifestations,

Have agreed on the following:

PART I

ARTICLE 1. Discrimination
For the purposes of the present Convention, the term "discrimination against women" shall mean any distinction, exclusion or restriction made on the basis of sex which has the effect or purpose of impairing or nullifying the recognition, enjoyment or exercise by women irrespective of their marital status, on a basis of equality of men and women, of human rights and fundamental freedoms in the political, economic, social, cultural, civil or any other field.

ARTICLE 2. Policy Measures
States Parties condemn discrimination against women in all its forms, agree to pursue by all appropriate means and without delay a policy of eliminating discrimination against women and, to this end, undertake:
   a. To embody the principle of the equality of men and women in their national constitutions or other appropriate legislation if not yet incorporated therein and to ensure, through law and other appropriate means, the practical realization of this principle;
   b. To adopt appropriate legislative and other measures, including sanctions where appropriate, prohibiting all discrimination against women;
   c. To establish legal protection of the rights of women on an equal basis with men and to ensure through competent national tribunals and other public institutions the effective protection of women against any act of discrimination;
   d. To refrain from engaging in any act or practice of discrimination against women and to ensure that public authorities and institutions shall act in conformity with this obligation;
   e. To take all appropriate measures to eliminate discrimination against women by any person, organization or enterprise;
   f. To take all appropriate measures, including legislation, to modify or abolish existing laws, regulations, customs and practices which constitute discrimination against women;
   g. To repeal all national penal provisions which constitute discrimination against women.

ARTICLE 3. Guarantee of Basic Human Rights and Fundamental Freedoms
States Parties shall take in all fields, in particular in the political, social, economic and cultural fields, all appropriate measures, including legislation, to ensure the full development and advancement of women, for the purpose of guaranteeing them the exercise and enjoyment of human rights and fundamental freedoms on a basis of equality with men.

ARTICLE 4. Special Measures
1. Adoption by States Parties of temporary special measures aimed at accelerating de facto equality between men and women shall not be considered discrimination as defined in the present Convention, but shall in no way entail as a consequence the maintenance of unequal or separate standards; these measures shall be discontinued when the objectives of equality of opportunity and treatment have been achieved.
2. Adoption by States Parties of special measures, including those measures contained in the present Convention, aimed at protecting maternity shall not be considered discriminatory.

ARTICLE 5. Sex Role Stereotyping and Prejudice
States Parties shall take all appropriate measures:
   a. To modify the social and cultural patterns of conduct of men and women, with a view to achieving the elimination of prejudices and customary and all other practices which are based on the idea of the inferiority or the superiority of either of the sexes or on stereotyped roles for men and women;
   b. To ensure that family education includes a proper understanding of maternity as a social function and the recognition of the common responsibility of men and women in the upbringing and development of their children, it being understood that the interest of the children is the primordial consideration in all cases.

ARTICLE 6. Prostitution
States Parties shall take all appropriate measures, including legislation, to suppress all forms of traffic in women and exploitation of prostitution of women.

PART II

ARTICLE 7.

States Parties shall take all appropriate measures to eliminate discrimination against women in the political and public life of the country and, in particular, shall ensure to women, on equal terms with men, the right:

   a. To vote in all elections and public referenda and to be eligible for election to all publicly elected bodies;
   b. To participate in the formulation of government policy and the implementation thereof and to hold public office and perform all public functions at all levels of government;
   c. To participate in non-governmental organizations and associations concerned with the public and political life of the country.

ARTICLE 8.

States Parties shall take all appropriate measures to ensure to women, on equal terms with men and without any discrimination, the opportunity to represent their Governments at the international level and to participate in the work of international organizations.

ARTICLE 9.

1. States Parties shall grant women equal rights with men to acquire, change or retain their nationality. They shall ensure in particular that neither marriage to an alien nor change of nationality by the husband during marriage shall automatically change the nationality of the wife, render her stateless or force upon her the nationality of the husband.
2. States Parties shall grant women equal rights with men with respect to the nationality of their children.

PART III

ARTICLE 10.

States Parties shall take all appropriate measures to eliminate discrimination against women in order to ensure to them equal rights with men in the field of education and in particular to ensure, on a basis of equality of men and women:

   a. The same conditions for career and vocational guidance, for access to studies and for the achievement of diplomas in educational establishments of all categories in rural as well as in urban areas; this equality shall be ensured in preschool, general, technical, professional and higher technical education, as well as in all types of vocational training;
   b. Access to the same curricula, the same examinations, teaching staff with qualifications of the same standard and school premises and equipment of the same quality;
   c. The elimination of any stereotyped concept of the roles of men and women at all levels and in all forms of education by encouraging coeducation and other types of education which will help to achieve this aim and, in particular, by the revision of textbooks and school programmes and the adaptation of teaching methods;
   d. The same opportunities to benefit from scholarships and other study grants;
   e. The same opportunities for access to programmes of continuing education including adult and functional literacy programmes, particularly those aimed at reducing, at the earliest possible time, any gap in education existing between men and women;
   f. The reduction of female student drop-out rates and the organization of programmes for girls and women who have left school prematurely;
   g. The same opportunities to participate actively in sports and physical education;
   h. Access to specific educational information to help to ensure the health and well-being of families, including information and advice on family planning.

ARTICLE 11.

1. States Parties shall take all appropriate measures to eliminate discrimination against women in the field of employment in order to ensure, on a basis of equality of men and women, the same rights, in particular:

   a. The right to work as an inalienable right of all human beings;
   b. The right to the same employment opportunities, including the application of the same criteria for selection in mat-

ters of employment;
- c. The right to free choice of profession and employment, the right to promotion, job security and all benefits and conditions of service and the right to receive vocational training and retraining, including apprenticeships, advanced vocational training and recurrent training;
- d. The right to equal remuneration, including benefits, and to equal treatment in respect of work of equal value, as well as equality of treatment in the evaluation of the quality of work;
- e. The right to social security, particularly in cases of retirement, unemployment, sickness, invalidity and old age and other incapacity to work, as well as the right to paid leave;
- f. The right to protection of health and to safety in working conditions, including the safeguarding of the function of reproduction.

2. In order to prevent discrimination against women on the grounds of marriage or maternity and to ensure their effective right to work, States Parties shall take appropriate measures:
   - a. To prohibit, subject to the imposition of sanctions, dismissal on the grounds of pregnancy or of maternity leave and discrimination in dismissals on the basis of marital status;
   - b. To introduce maternity leave with pay or with comparable social benefits without loss of former employment, seniority or social allowances;
   - c. To encourage the provision of the necessary supporting social services to enable parents to combine family obligations with work responsibilities and participation in public life, in particular through promoting the establishment and development of a network of child-care facilities;
   - d. To provide special protection to women during pregnancy in types of work proved to be harmful to them.

3. Protective legislation relating to matters covered in this article shall be reviewed periodically in the light of scientific and technological knowledge and shall be revised, repealed or extended as necessary.

ARTICLE 12.

1. States Parties shall take all appropriate measures to eliminate discrimination against women in the field of health care in order to ensure, on a basis of equality of men and women, access to health care services, including those related to family planning.
2. Notwithstanding the provisions of paragraph 1 of this article, States Parties shall ensure to women appropriate services in connection with pregnancy, confinement and the post-natal period, granting free services where necessary, as well as adequate nutrition during pregnancy and lactation.

ARTICLE 13.

States Parties shall take all appropriate measures to eliminate discrimination against women in other areas of economic and social life in order to ensure, on a basis of equality of men and women, the same rights, in particular:
- a. The right to family benefits;
- b. The right to bank loans, mortgages and other forms of financial credit;
- c. The right to participate in recreational activities, sports and all aspects of cultural life.

ARTICLE 14.

1. States Parties shall take into account the particular problems faced by rural women and the significant roles which rural women play in the economic survival of their families, including their work in the non-monetized sectors of the economy, and shall take all appropriate measures to ensure the application of the provisions of this Convention to women in rural areas.
2. States Parties shall take all appropriate measures to eliminate discrimination against women in rural areas in order to ensure, on a basis of equality of men and women, that they participate in and benefit from rural development and, in particular, shall ensure to such women the right:
   - a. To participate in the elaboration and implementation of development planning at all levels;
   - b. To have access to adequate health care facilities, including information, counselling and services in family planning;
   - c. To benefit directly from social security programmes;
   - d. To obtain all types of training and education, formal and non-formal, including that relating to functional literacy, as well as, inter alia, the benefit of all community and extension services, in order to increase their technical proficiency;
   - e. To organize self-help groups and co-operatives in order to obtain equal access to economic opportunities through employment or self-employment;

- f. To participate in all community activities;
- g. To have access to agricultural credit and loans, marketing facilities, appropriate technology and equal treatment in land and agrarian reform as well as in land resettlement schemes;
- h. To enjoy adequate living conditions, particularly in relation to housing, sanitation, electricity and water supply, transport and communications.

PART IV

ARTICLE 15.

1. States Parties shall accord to women equality with men before the law.
2. States Parties shall accord to women, in civil matters, a legal capacity identical to that of men and the same opportunities to exercise that capacity. In particular, they shall give women equal rights to conclude contracts and to administer property and shall treat them equally in all stages of procedure in courts and tribunals.
3. States Parties agree that all contracts and all other private instruments of any kind with a legal effect which is directed at restricting the legal capacity of women shall be deemed null and void.
4. States Parties shall accord to men and women the same rights with regard to the law relating to the movement of persons and the freedom to choose their residence and domicile.

ARTICLE 16.

1. States Parties shall take all appropriate measures to eliminate discrimination against women in all matters relating to marriage and family relations and in particular shall ensure, on a basis of equality of men and women:
   - a. The same right to enter into marriage;
   - b. The same right freely to choose a spouse and to enter into marriage only with their free and full consent;
   - c. The same rights and responsibilities during marriage and at its dissolution;
   - d. The same rights and responsibilities as parents, irrespective of their marital status, in matters relating to their children; in all cases the interests of the children shall be paramount;
   - e. The same rights to decide freely and responsibly on the number and spacing of their children and to have access to the information, education and means to enable them to exercise these rights;
   - f. The same rights and responsibilities with regard to guardianship, wardship, trusteeship and adoption of children, or similar institutions where these concepts exist in national legislation; in all cases the interests of the children shall be paramount;
   - g. The same personal rights as husband and wife, including the right to choose a family name, a profession and an occupation;
   - h. The same rights for both spouses in respect of the ownership, acquisition, management, administration, enjoyment and disposition of property, whether free of charge or for a valuable consideration.
2. The betrothal and the marriage of a child shall have no legal effect, and all necessary action, including legislation, shall be taken to specify a minimum age for marriage and to make the registration of marriages in an official registry compulsory.

PART V

ARTICLE 17.

1. For the purpose of considering the progress made in the implementation of the present Convention, there shall be established a Committee on the Elimination of Discrimination Against Women (hereinafter referred to as the Committee) consisting, at the time of entry into force of the Convention, of eighteen and, after ratification of or accession to the Convention by the thirty-fifth State Party, of twenty-three experts of high moral standing and competence in the field covered by the Convention. The experts shall be elected by States Parties from among their nationals and shall serve in their personal capacity, consideration being given to equitable geographical distribution and to the representation of the different forms of civilization as well as the principal legal systems.
2. The members of the Committee shall be elected by secret ballot from a list of persons nominated by States Parties. Each State Party may nominate one person from among its own nationals.
3. The initial election shall be held six months after the date of the entry into force of the present Convention. At least three

months before the date of each election the Secretary-General of the United Nations shall address a letter to the States Parties inviting them to submit their nominations within two months. The Secretary-General shall prepare a list in alphabetical order of all persons thus nominated, indicating the States Parties which have nominated them, and shall submit it to the States Parties.

4. Elections of the members of the Committee shall be held at a meeting of States Parties convened by the Secretary-General at United Nations Headquarters. At that meeting, for which two thirds of the States Parties shall constitute a quorum, the persons elected to the Committee shall be those nominees who obtain the largest number of votes and an absolute majority of the votes of the representatives of States Parties present and voting.

5. The members of the Committee shall be elected for a term of four years. However, the terms of nine of the members elected at the first election shall expire at the end of two years; immediately after the first election the names of these nine members shall be chosen by lot by the Chairman of the Committee.

6. The election of the five additional members of the Committee shall be held in accordance with the provisions of paragraphs 2, 3 and 4 of this article, following the thirty-fifth ratification or accession. The terms of two of the additional members elected on this occasion shall expire at the end of two years, the names of these two members having been chosen by lot by the Chairman of the Committee.

7. For the filling of casual vacancies, the State Party whose expert has ceased to function as a member of the Committee shall appoint another expert from among its nationals, subject to the approval of the Committee.

8. The members of the Committee shall, with the approval of the General Assembly, receive emoluments from United Nations resources on such terms and conditions as the Assembly may decide, having regard to the importance of the Committee's responsibilities.

9. The Secretary-General of the United Nations shall provide the necessary staff and facilities for the effective performance of the functions of the Committee under the present Convention.

ARTICLE 18.

1. States Parties undertake to submit to the Secretary-General of the United Nations, for consideration by the Committee, a report on the legislative, judicial, administrative or other measures which they have adopted to give effect to the provisions of the present Convention and on the progress made in this respect:
   a. Within one year after the entry into force for the State concerned; and
   b. Thereafter at least every four years and further whenever the Committee so requests.
2. Reports may indicate factors and difficulties affecting the degree of fulfilment of obligations under the present Convention.

ARTICLE 19.

1. The Committee shall adopt its own rules of procedure.
2. The Committee shall elect its officers for a term of two years.

ARTICLE 20.

1. The Committee shall normally meet for a period of not more than two weeks annually in order to consider the reports submitted in accordance with article 18 of the present Convention.
2. The meetings of the Committee shall normally be held at United Nations Headquarters or at any other convenient place as determined by the Committee.

ARTICLE 21.

1. The Committee shall, through the Economic and Social Council, report annually to the General Assembly of the United Nations on its activities and may make suggestions and general recommendations based on the examination of reports and information received from the States Parties. Such suggestions and general recommendations shall be included in the report of the Committee together with comments, if any, from States Parties.
2. The Secretary-General shall transmit the reports of the Committee to the Commission on the Status of Women for its information.

ARTICLE 22.

The specialized agencies shall be entitled to be represented at the consideration of the implementation of such provisions of the present Convention as fall within the scope of their activities. The Committee may invite the specialized agencies to submit reports on the implementation of the Convention in areas falling within the scope of their activities.

PART VI

ARTICLE 23.
Nothing in this Convention shall affect any provisions that are more conducive to the achievement of equality between men and women which may be contained:
   a. In the legislation of a State Party; or
   b. In any other international convention, treaty or agreement in force for that State.

ARTICLE 24.
States Parties undertake to adopt all necessary measures at the national level aimed at achieving the full realization of the rights recognized in the present Convention.

ARTICLE 25.
1. The present Convention shall be open for signature by all States.
2. The Secretary-General of the United Nations is designated as the depositary of the present Convention.
3. The present Convention is subject to ratification. Instruments of ratification shall be deposited with the Secretary-General of the United Nations.
4. The present Convention shall be open to accession by all States. Accession shall be effected by the deposit of an instrument of accession with the Secretary-General of the United Nations.

ARTICLE 26.
1. A request for the revision of the present Convention may be made at any time by any State Party by means of a notification in writing addressed to the Secretary-General of the United Nations.
2. The General Assembly of the United Nations shall decide upon the steps, if any, to be taken in respect of such a request.

ARTICLE 27.
1. The present Convention shall enter into force on the thirtieth day after the date of deposit with the Secretary-General of the United Nations of the twentieth instrument of ratification or accession.
2. For each State ratifying the present Convention or acceding to it after the deposit of the twentieth instrument of ratification or accession, the Convention shall enter into force on the thirtieth day after the date of the deposit of its own instrument of ratification or accession.

ARTICLE 28.
1. The Secretary-General of the United Nations shall receive and circulate to all States the text of reservations made by States at the time of ratification or accession.
2. A reservation incompatible with the object and purpose of the present Convention shall not be permitted.
3. Reservations may be withdrawn at any time by notification to this effect addressed to the Secretary-General of the United Nations, who shall then inform all States thereof. Such notification shall take effect on the date on which it is received.

ARTICLE 29.
1. Any dispute between two or more States Parties concerning the interpretation or application of the present Convention which is not settled by negotiation shall, at the request of one of them, be submitted to arbitration. If within six months from the date of the request for arbitration the parties are unable to agree on the organization of the arbitration, any one of those parties may refer the dispute to the International Court of Justice by request in conformity with the Statute of the Court.
2. Each State Party may at the time of signature or ratification of this Convention or accession thereto declare that it does not consider itself bound by paragraph 1 of this article. The other States Parties shall not be bound by that paragraph with respect to any State Party which has made such a reservation.
3. Any State Party which has made a reservation in accordance with paragraph 2 of this article may at any time withdraw that reservation by notification to the Secretary-General of the United Nations.

Anatomy of the Beijing Platform for Action

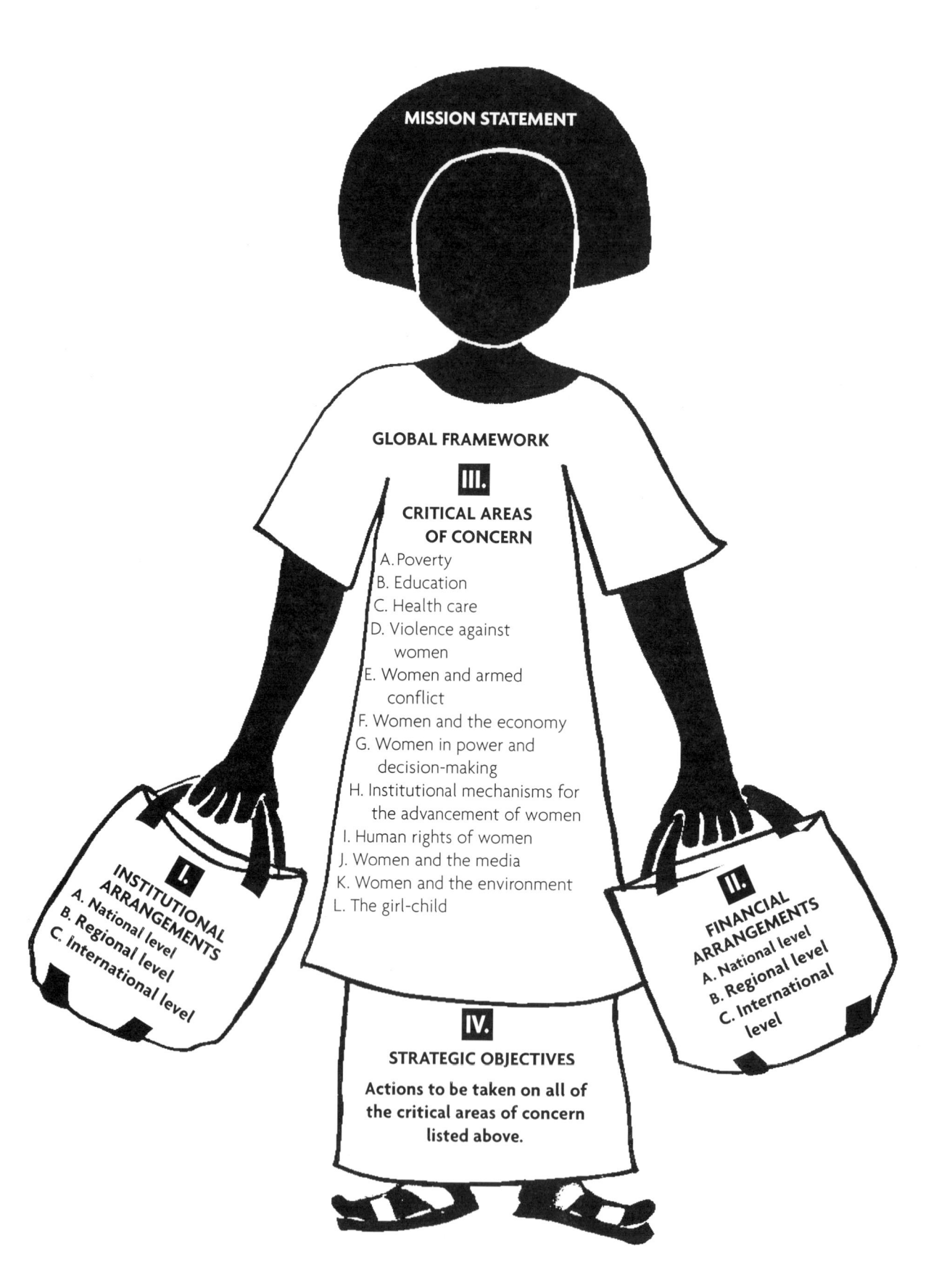

MISSION STATEMENT

GLOBAL FRAMEWORK

III.

CRITICAL AREAS OF CONCERN

A. Poverty
B. Education
C. Health care
D. Violence against women
E. Women and armed conflict
F. Women and the economy
G. Women in power and decision-making
H. Institutional mechanisms for the advancement of women
I. Human rights of women
J. Women and the media
K. Women and the environment
L. The girl-child

I.

INSTITUTIONAL ARRANGEMENTS
A. National level
B. Regional level
C. International level

II.

FINANCIAL ARRANGEMENTS
A. National level
B. Regional level
C. International level

IV.

STRATEGIC OBJECTIVES

Actions to be taken on all of the critical areas of concern listed above.

The Beijing Platform for Action at a Glance

The Platform for Action is an international guideline for women's policies. It outlines many of the emerging rights we've discussed earlier in the book. Here is an abbreviation of the key actions to be taken by governments in the twelve critical areas of concern.

PLATFORM FOR ACTION
Strategic Objectives and Actions (Chapter IV)

A. Women and Poverty
1. Review, adopt and maintain macroeconomic policies and development strategies that address the needs and efforts of women in poverty.
2. Revise laws and administrative practices to ensure women's equal rights and access to economic resources.
3. Provide women with access to savings and credit mechanisms and institutions.
4. Develop gender-based methodologies and conduct research to address the feminization of poverty.

B. Education and training of women
1. Ensure equal access to education.
2. Eradicate illiteracy among women.
3. Improve women's access to vocational training, science and technology, and continuing education.
4. Develop non-discriminatory education and training.
5. Allocate sufficient resources for and monitor the implementation of educational reforms.
6. Promote lifelong education and training for girls and women.

C. Women and health
1. Increase women's access throughout their life cycle to appropriate, affordable and quality health care, information and related services.
2. Strengthen preventive programmes that promote women's health.
3. Undertake gender-sensitive initiatives that address sexually transmitted diseases, HIV/AIDS and sexual and reproductive health issues.
4. Promote research and disseminate information on women's health.
5. Increase resources and monitor follow-up for women's health.

D. Violence against women
1. Take integrated measures to prevent and eliminate violence against women.
2. Study the causes and consequences of violence against women and the effectiveness of preventive measures.
3. Eliminate trafficking in women and assist victims of violence due to prostitution and trafficking.

E. Women and armed conflict
1. Increase the participation of women in conflict resolution at decision-making levels and protect women living in situations of armed and other conflict or under foreign occupation.
2. Reduce excessive military expenditures and control the availability of armaments.
3. Promote non-violent forms of conflict resolution and reduce the incidence of human rights abuse in conflict situations.
4. Promote women's contribution to fostering a culture of peace.
5. Provide protection, assistance and training to refugee women, other displaced women in need of international protection and internally displaced women.
6. Provide assistance to the women of the colonies and non-self-governing territories.

F. Women and the economy
1. Promote women's economic rights and independence, including access to employment and appropriate working conditions and control over economic resources.
2. Facilitate women's equal access to resources, employment, markets and trade.
3. Provide business services, training and access to markets, information and technology, particularly to low-income women.
4. Strengthen women's economic capacity and commercial networks.
5. Eliminate occupational segregation and all forms of discrimination.
6. Promote harmonization of work and family responsibilities for women and men.

G. Women in power and decision-making
1. Take measures to ensure women's equal access to and full participation in power structures and decision-making.
2. Increase women's capacity to participate in decision-making and leadership.

H. Institutional mechanisms for the advancement of women
1. Create or strengthen national machineries and other governmental bodies that advance women.
2. Integrate gender perspectives in legislation, public policies, programmes and projects.
3. Generate and disseminate gender-aggregated data and information for planning and evaluation.

I. Human rights of women
1. Promote and protect the human rights of women through the full implementation of all human rights instruments, especially the Convention on the Elimination of All Forms of Discrimination Against Women.
2. Ensure equality and non-discrimination under the law and in practice.
3. Achieve legal literacy.

J. Women and the media
1. Increase the participation and access of women to expression and decision-making in and through the media and new technologies of communication.
2. Encourage and recognize women's media networks, including electronic networks and other new technologies of communication, as a means for the dissemination of information and the exchange of views, including at the international level, and support women's groups active in all media work and systems of communication to that end.
3. Promote a balanced and non-stereotyped portrayal of women in the media.

K. Women and the environment
1. Involve women actively in environmental decision-making at all levels.
2. Integrate gender concerns and perspectives in policies and programmes for sustainable development.
3. Strengthen or establish mechanisms at the national, regional and international levels to assess the impact of development and environmental policies on women.

L. The girl-child
1. Eliminate all forms of discrimination against the girl-child.
2. Eliminate negative cultural attitudes and practices against girls.
3. Promote and protect the rights of the girl-child and increase awareness of her needs and potential.
4. Eliminate discrimination against girls in education, skills development and training.
5. Eliminate discrimination against girls in health and nutrition.
6. Eliminate the economic exploitation of child labour and protect young girls at work.
7. Eradicate violence against the girl-child.
8. Promote the girl-child's awareness of and participation in social, economic and political life.
9. Strengthen the role of the the family in improving the status of the girl-child.

International Women's Tribune Centre

International Women's Tribune Centre
777 United Nations Plaza
New York
NY 10017, USA
Tel: 1-212-687-8633
Fax: 1-212-661-2704
E-mail: iwtc@igc.apc.org

STAFF
IWTC
Anne S. Walker
Vicki J. Semler
Alice Quinn
Vanessa Davis
Yolande Atwater
Women, Ink.
Tina Johnson
Mary Wong
Steve Vingelli

TO ORDER BOOKS OR FOR OUR FREE CATALOGUE, CONTACT:
Women, Ink.
777 United Nations Plaza
New York
NY 10017, USA
Tel: 212-687-8633
Fax: 212-661-2704
E-mail: wink@womenink.org
Web site: www.womenink.org

The International Women's Tribune Centre (IWTC) is an international NGO whose purpose is to promote the increased participation of women in shaping and redefining a development process that is participatory, holistic and inclusive. The organization's work reflects a convergence of its roots and roles in two arenas: the international women's movement and the development community. IWTC's programmes are based on the belief that accessible information and participatory processes are essential to development and are at the heart of the growing global women's movement.

Working in collaboration with women's organizations in the Global South, IWTC uses information, education, communication and organizing skills and strategies to convert research, policy and ideas into action. It offers workshops and technical support, produces training manuals and other educational materials, provides networking and information-brokering services and fosters linkages between the international and the national, between the abstract and the practical, between the governmental and the non-governmental.

IWTC produces a women and development newsletter, *The Tribune*, and the bi-weekly *Women's GlobalNet*, a one-page bulletin of up-to-the minute information on activities and initiatives of women worldwide, sent via fax and e-mail to tens of thousands of individuals and groups in every world region. All IWTC's materials are free to individuals and groups in the Global South.

Women, Ink.

A project of IWTC, Women, Ink. is a book marketing and distribution initiative offering "one-stop shopping" for the best and latest books in gender and development from more than 90 publishers and organizations worldwide. Its collection of 250 titles encompasses issues ranging from Gender Analysis and Planning and Women's Human Rights to Structural Adjustment and Natural Resource Management. Women, Ink. is the exclusive distributor of the United Nations Development Fund for Women (UNIFEM) publications and provides an international outlet for publications by small presses and women's organizations in the Global South.

The list of titles on the opposite page is only a small selection of what is in the free catalogue, available on request. Women, Ink. also has a Web site at <www.womenink.org> which is secured for credit card ordering on-line.

WOMEN, INK. RESOURCES

THE FOLLOWING TITLES MENTIONED IN THIS MANUAL ARE AVAILABLE FROM WOMEN, INK.
(See page number for description)

Across Borders: Women with Disabilities Working Together. Diane Driedger, Irene Reika & Eileen Girón *(p. 75)*

Advocacy Kit on CEDAW. *(p. 23)*

The Burden of Girlhood: A Global Inquiry into the Status of Girls. Neera Kuckreja Sohoni *(p. 39)*

Choose a Future: Issues and Options for Adolescent Girls. *(p. 39)*

Claiming Our Place: Working the Human Rights System to Women's Advantage. Margaret A. Schuler (Ed.) *(p. 23)*

Demanding Accountability: The Global Campaign and the Vienna Tribunal for Women's Human Rights. Charlotte Bunch & Niamh Reilly *(p. 102)*

Ecofeminism. Marie Mies and Vandana Shiva *(p. 72)*

Ecofeminism: Women, Culture, Nature. Karen J. Warren (Ed.) *(p. 72)*

Empowerment: Towards Sustainable Development. Naresh Singh & Vangile Titi (Eds.) *(p. 72)*

Female Genital Mutilation: A Call to Global Action. Nahid Toubia *(p. 66)*

Gender and Disability: Women's Experiences in the Middle East. Lina Abu-Habib *(p. 75)*

Gender and Sustainable Development. Ana Maria Brasileiro (Ed.) *(p. 72)*

Gender in Popular Education: Methods for Empowerment. Shirley Walters & Linzi Manicom (Eds.) *(p. 31)*

Gender Justice: Women's Rights Are Human Rights Elizabeth Fisher and Linda Gray MacKay *(p. 23)*

Gender Violence and Women's Human Rights in Africa. Center for Women's Global Leadership *(p. 66)*

Gender, Work and Tourism. M. Thea Sinclair (Ed.) *(p. 35)*

Globalization, Adult Education and Training. Shirley Walters (Ed.) *(p. 31)*

Homeworkers in Global Perspective: Invisible No More. Eileen Boris & Elisabeth Prügl (Eds.) *(p. 35)*

Human Rights of Women: National and International Perspectives Rebecca J. Cook (Ed.) *(p. 23)*

The Human Rights Watch Global Report on Women's Rights. *(p. 43)*

Improving the Quality of Life of Girls. Kathleen M. Kurz & Cynthia J. Prather *(p. 39)*

It's About Time: Human Rights Are Women's Right. *(p. 43)*

Local Action/Global Change: Learning About the Human Rights of Women and Girls Julie Mertus with Malika Dutt & Nancy Flowers *(p. 23)*

Loud, Proud and Passionate: Including Women with Disabilities in International Development Programmes. *(p. 75)*

No Sweat: Fashion, Free Trade and the Rights of Garment Workers. Andrew Ross (Ed.) *(p. 35)*

Promoting Reproductive Rights: A Global Mandate. Reed Boland & Anika Rahman *(p. 69)*

Reproductive Rights in Practice. Anita Hardon & Elizabeth Hayes *(p. 69)*

The Right to Live Without Violence: Women's Proposals and Actions. Latin American & Caribbean Women's Health Network *(p. 102)*

The Right to Reproductive Choice: A Study in International Law. Corinne A. A. Packer *(p. 69)*

Women of the World: Formal Laws and Policies Affecting Their Reproductive Lives. CRLP *(p. 69)*

The State of Women in the World Atlas. Joni Seager *(p. 39)*

States Responses to Domestic Violence: Current Status and Needed Improvements. Women, Law & Development International *(p. 66)*

Stolen Lives: Trading Women into Sex and Slavery. Sietske Altink *(p. 49)*

The Traffic in Women: Human Realities of the International Sex Trade. Siriporn Skrobanek, Nattaya Boonpakdee & Chutima Jantateroo *(p. 49)*

STOP Female Genital Mutilation: Women Speak. Fran P. Hosken *(p. 66)*

Strategies for Confronting Domestic Violence: A Resource Manual. *(p. 66)*

Trafficking in Women: Forced Labour and Slavery-like Practices in Marriage, Domestic Labour and Prostitution. Marjan Wijers & Lin Lap-Chew *(p. 49)*

Unspoken Rules: Sexual Orientation and Women's Rights. Rachel Rosenbloom (Ed.) *(p. 76)*

Violence Against Women: New Movements and New Theories in India. Gail Omvedt *(p. 66)*

Where Women Stand: An International Report on the Status of Women in 140 Countries. Naomi Neft & Ann D. Levine *(p. 39)*

Without Reservation: The Beijing Tribunal on Accountability for Women's Human Rights. Niamh Reilly (Ed.) *(p. 102)*

Women Against Violence: Breaking the Silence. Ana Maria Brasileiro (Ed.) *(p. 66)*

Women and Literacy. Marcella Ballara *(p. 31)*

Women and Sustainable Development in Africa. Valentine Udoh James (Ed.) *(p. 72)*

Women and the University Curriculum: Towards Equality, Democracy and Peace. Mary Louise Kearney & Anne Holden Rønning (Eds.) *(p. 31)*

Women and Violence: Realities and Responses Worldwide. Miranda Davies (Ed.) *(p. 66)*

Women, Employment and Exclusion. Caroline Sweetman (Ed.) *(p. 35)*

Women's Guide to the Wired World. Shana Penn *(p. 124)*

Women's Human Rights Step by Step: A Practical Guide for Using International Human Rights Law. *(p. 23)*

Women's Rights, Human Rights: International Feminist Perspectives. Andrea Wolper & Julie S. Peters *(p. 49)*

WOW: Women on the Web. Helen Fallon *(p. 124)*

RESOURCE KIT **147**

WOMEN, INK. ORDER FORM

COMPLETE TITLE	PRICE (US$)	QTY	TOTAL
ACROSS BORDERS: Women with Disabilities (EXAMPLE)	14.95	2	29.90

Please continue your order on another sheet of paper if you are ordering more than 7 titles.

Subtotal

Shipping/handling (see below)

TOTAL

Orders from individuals and all overseas customers must be prepaid to *Women, Ink.* by: Cheque (US dollars drawn on US bank), International money order in US dollars, Direct deposit into *Women, Ink.* bank account (Chase Bank, New York: #152-012761), or credit card (MasterCard/Visa). For fastest service, order by phone or on-line (credit card holders only).

☐ VISA   ☐ MasterCard   *(minimum order for credit cards is US$15.00 excluding postage)*

Card number ☐☐☐☐☐☐☐☐☐☐☐☐☐☐☐☐   Exp. Date ___/___

Name on card (please print) _____

Signature _____

Tel: (_____) _____   Fax: (_____) _____

BILLING ADDRESS: (please print)

Name _____   Organization: _____

Street Address _____

City _____ State _____ Post Code _____ Country _____

SHIPPING ADDRESS (if different from above):

Name _____   Organization _____

Street Address _____

City _____ State _____ Post Code _____ Country _____

Shipping and Handling Charges

	Surface	Air		Surface	Air
United States, Canada & Mexico	$5.00 first♦ $2.00/add'l	$9.50 first◇ $3.00/add'l	Caribbean, Central America	$6.00 first $3.00/add'l	$10.00 first $4.50/add'l
Europe, UK & S. America	$6.50 first $3.50/add'l	$12.00 first $5.00/add'l	Africa, Asia & Pacific	$7.00 first $3.00/add'l	$16.00 first $8.50/add'l

Key: ♦=UPS   ◇=2nd Day Air

WOMEN, INK.
777 United Nations Plaza
New York, NY 10017, USA
Tel: 1-212-687-8633
Fax: 1-212-661-2704
E-mail:<wink@womenink.org>
Web site: www.womenink.org